PARANORMAL
WALES

MARK REES

Acknowledgements

Thank you to everyone who has joined me on this journey into the darkest depths of Wales' haunted heritage. In particular, I would like to wish a huge *diolch o'r galon* to my family for their continued support, and to all at Amberley Publishing for commissioning the book which you now hold in your hands.

The world of the paranormal is full of wonderfully passionate people, many of whom have supported me not only in researching my books, but also at my events and talks. I have made some great friends along the way and am eternally grateful to all who answered my requests for information, spoke about their personal experiences, and suggested ideas of their own.

This book would not have been possible without the help of a great number of people who are mentioned throughout, and I would also like to thank Emma Hardy, *The Bay* magazine, The Comix Shoppe, Cymru Paranormal, Sandra Evans and Dan Turner, Fluellen Theatre Company, Folklore Thursday, Phil Hoyles, Robert King, Rod Lloyd, the Lotus Sisters, Gareth Maund, Media Wales, Karl Morgan and all at Swansea Museum, Owen Staton, Wyn Thomas, my footballing companions Jean and Lindsay, and you, dear reader, for picking up this diabolical tome.

First published 2020

Amberley Publishing
The Hill, Stroud
Gloucestershire, GL5 4EP

www.amberley-books.com

Copyright © Mark Rees, 2020

The right of Mark Rees to be identified as the Author
of this work has been asserted in accordance with the
Copyrights, Designs and Patents Act 1988.

All rights reserved. No part of this book may be reprinted or reproduced
or utilised in any form or by any electronic, mechanical or other means,
now known or hereafter invented, including photocopying and recording,
or in any information storage or retrieval system, without the permission
in writing from the Publishers.

British Library Cataloguing in Publication Data.
A catalogue record for this book is available from the British Library.

ISBN 978 1 4456 9716 1 (print)
ISBN 978 1 4456 9717 8 (ebook)

Typesetting by Aura Technology and Software Services, India.
Printed in Great Britain.

Contents

	Introduction	5
1	Creepy Castles	7
2	Haunted History	25
3	Pubs and Hotels	40
4	Grand Mansions	58
5	Cultural Landmarks	73
	Bibliography	94
	About the Author	96

Introduction

Many years ago, I spent the night in one of Wales' 'most haunted' locations. I was joined by a group of like-minded media people to write a Halloween report for a glossy magazine, and as the shades of night fell we experienced the whole gamut of supernatural activity commonly associated with such affairs. Objects were thrown, bangs were heard, and the glass whizzed around the Ouija board to offer up all manner of obscure communications from beyond.

Did we encounter anything genuinely paranormal? I have no idea, but while some of the more faint-hearted members of the party gave up the ghost and fled for safety, I was hooked. Little did I know, however, that I would soon be travelling the length and breadth of the country to repeat the experience and, best of all, even writing books on the subject.

The ghosts of Wales are nothing if not varied, and many of the traditional stories are firmly steeped in myths and legends. They are spooky yarns of restless monks who continue to worship in their ivy-strewn abbeys, knights in shining armour who clank around Gothic fortresses, and spectral ladies with a penchant for dressing in a single colour.

On the other hand, there are numerous contemporary reports that are far more grounded in reality and, some might say, are much more terrifying as a result. The entries contained within this book aim to reflect the wide range of accounts available, and by looking at the tales of old alongside modern-day sightings, connections might emerge that link the more superstitiously minded past to the more scientifically minded present.

My research was sourced from a wide range of places, and for the historical accounts I am indebted to those writers who trod a similar path before me. They include nineteenth-century pioneers such as Wirt Sikes, who deemed the traditional folk tales worthy of preserving, to twentieth-century trailblazers like Peter Underwood, who conceived of the idea of regional- and country-specific ghost books, such as the one that you now hold in your hands.

The more recent accounts have been gathered from news articles, many of which I wrote myself during my time working for the press, and by doing some good old-fashioned journalism, which involved chatting with the locals and interviewing those involved. I also had a first-hand insight into the methods of modern-day ghost hunting thanks to the paranormal groups who kindly invited me along on their investigations. In particular, Cymru Paranormal went above and beyond in their assistance, and their support and friendship has been invaluable.

There are hundreds of supposedly haunted places all across Wales and, as such, this book is far from a comprehensive list. If I had attempted such a monumental task I would still be writing it now, and so a selection process had to be decided upon.

To begin with, it was important to reflect the country as a whole, and not just those counties that are overly blessed with spook-infested properties. This is why you will find entries that span from the furthest tip of Anglesey protruding out into the Irish Sea, to those just a stone's throw away from the English border along the River Wye. Also, in order to avoid dwelling on a certain type of building, such as castles of which there are an abundance, I divided this book into five roughly equal-sized sections, which range from grand stately homes to long-standing watering holes.

As a result, some of your favourite places – along with some of mine – might have just missed out. This is something that I hope to address in future volumes.

Finally, it is my hope that this book will serve as a practical guidebook of sorts and, with this in mind, I wanted to include entries that still exist today and, ideally, can be easily visited by those who have their curiosity piqued. Wherever you might find yourself in Wales, this tome should provide you with everything you need to set off on an adventure of your own, be that by simply having a quick drink in an atmospheric pub, or by immersing yourself in the full experience with an overnight vigil at one of Wales' 'most haunted' locations. Be warned, however, once you catch that paranormal bug, it can become a life-long obsession!

Happy hunting.

Mark Rees, 2020

CHAPTER ONE

Creepy Castles

Wales, it is said, is home to more castles per square mile than any other country in the world. With countless tales of ghostly goings on attached to their time-ravaged walls, it could also lay claim to being home to more haunted castles per square mile than any other country in the world as well. An estimated 600 of these once-mighty fortresses can be found across the land, and with around 100 of them still standing today, they are just waiting for modern-day visitors to cross their drawbridges and discover their spooky secrets.

Cardiff Castle, Castle Street, Cardiff

Cardiff Castle stands tall in the centre of Wales' capital city. The medieval fortress has long been one of the county's most recognisable attractions, but what the tourists who flock through its doors might be unaware of are the many strange accounts of shadowy figures, phantom women, and even poltergeist activity that have been reported within its historic walls.

Cardiff Castle.
(© Dun.can (CC BY 2.0))

The mansion at Cardiff Castle. (© Mario Sánchez Prada (CC BY-SA 2.0))

The keep at Cardiff Castle. (© Michel Curi (CC BY 2.0))

Above left: The bust inside Cardiff Castle. (© Ryan Kilpatrick (CC BY-ND 2.0))

Above right: Cardiff Castle's clock tower. (© Jon Candy (CC BY-SA 2.0))

The castle can trace its roots back some 2,000 years, having started life as a Roman fort on which a Norman motte-and-bailey castle was built. It was fortified in stone and further developed throughout the centuries, before falling into the hands of the Stuart dynasty in the eighteenth century.

Successive Marquesses of Bute transformed the crumbling ruin into the majestic home that we see today, and it was in the late Victorian period that John Crichton-Stuart, 3rd Marquess of Bute, enlisted the services of William Burges to work his magic on its mansion. The highly imaginative architect drew inspiration from the Gothic Revival movement to add a touch of romanticism to its many rooms, and was also responsible for reviving another of Bute's reputedly haunted castles, the nearby Castell Coch.

Following the death of the 4th Marquess in 1947, the family home passed into the care of the city of Cardiff. If the reports are to be believed, however, at least one its former owners still resides there today. In *Ghosts' Who's Who*, published in 1977, Jack Hallam wrote that the castle's custodian of fifteen years had personally seen two ghosts while on duty, that of a woman in a long robe, and a man believed to be the 2nd Marquess of Bute. The marquess died suddenly after a banquet in 1848, and is said to appear in the small room in which he passed away, a dressing room that was converted into a chapel. The exact spot is marked by a bust of his likeness, and from there he is said to wander into the adjacent library, with contemporary reports adding that he also passes through the walls and the fireplace.

One theory as to the identity of the woman is that she could be the restless spirit of Lady Sophia Rawdon-Hastings, the marquess' second wife, who, it would appear, continues to bear a grudge in the afterlife. Described as something of a 'difficult' person to live with, she is said to have been far from impressed with her husband's decision to be buried with his first wife when the fateful day arrived.

Lady Sophia might also have a family connection with possibly the most well known of the castle's night-time visitors. For centuries, a phantom horse and carriage has been reported charging at speed along the city's streets from the direction of Cardiff Bridge, before clattering through the gates and coming to a halt in the courtyard. Witnesses have described hearing the thunder of hooves and the bellow of a coachman urging it onwards, and its appearance is said to be a bad omen for the Hastings, as it signifies an imminent death in the family.

Another phantom that crosses the bridge, albeit in the opposite direction, is the so-called grey lady. She is described as being dressed from head to toe in a grey robe and hood, and has been seen waving as if to somebody in the tower. One of the earliest and more high-profile captives to be held in the castle was Robert Curthose, the son of William the Conqueror, who was imprisoned there for the last eight years of his life. It has been suggested that the grey lady might be trying to catch his attention, and has been spotted in the daytime as well as the night. Her route begins in what is now Queen Street, from where she walks through the city, past the castle, before coming to a halt on the bridge that crosses the River Taff. The ghost of a man seen inside the castle has also been attributed to the Duke of Normandy himself.

In more recent times, accounts of paranormal activity include the sound of footsteps and a sudden sense of dread, which is sometimes accompanied by an icy coldness. Shadow-like figures and an ethereal mist have been seen moving around the walls, while in the stockroom reports of loud noises and moving objects are thought to be the work of some unseen entity.

Kidwelly Castle, Castle Road, Kidwelly, Carmarthenshire

Kidwelly Castle is a romantic ruin that overlooks the flowing waters of the River Gwendraeth. It occupies an idyllic spot in the Carmarthenshire town of the same name, yet in days gone by it wasn't such a serene location, and witnessed many a bloody skirmish between the Welsh and the Norman invaders. It could also be the domain of the headless spirit of Wales' first 'warrior princess', who met with a gruesome fate following one such battle.

Now owned by CADW, the castle was built in the thirteenth century on the site of a twelfth-century fortress. It was during the Great Revolt in 1136 that Gwenllian, ferch Gruffydd (daughter of Gruffydd), led a spirited, if futile, rebellion against Maurice de Londres, the Lord of Kidwelly. With her husband Gruffudd ap Rhys, prince of Deheubarth, away rallying forces in the north, she received word of an imminent attack and hastily assembled an army in response. The gang of fighters, which included her two teenage sons, were no match for the Norman forces, who quickly crushed their resistance and captured Gwenllian. She was executed in a field outside the castle, which became known as Maes Gwenllian (Field of Gwenllian),

Kidwelly Castle on the River Gwendraeth. (© Colin (CC BY 2.0))

Kidwelly Castle gates. (© giborn_134 (CC BY-ND 2.0))

The inner ward at Kidwelly Castle. (© Steven Penton (CC BY 2.0))

Looking out at the fields from Kidwelly Castle. (© Tom Bastin (CC BY 2.0))

Inside Kidwelly Castle. (© Steven Penton (CC BY 2.0))

and according to local folklore, a spring appeared where her body fell. A memorial to the princess can now be seen outside the castle's great gatehouse.

Since those turbulent times there have been many reports of a decapitated entity walking the area at night, and in 1909 Marie Trevelyan published a description. She was said to be dressed in grey with a long trailing robe, a girdle, and a hood concealing her missing head. An 'old Carmarthenshire man' was even able to engage her in conversation, although how she spoke without a head is not explained. He asked her what she wanted, to which she replied: 'Alas! I cannot rest until I find my head. Help me to search for it.' This he did for more than an hour, and after failing to locate it returned on three consecutive nights until he found a stone that resembled a human skull in shape and size. He handed it to his companion, 'who concealed it under her robe, and hastened away.' With a replacement for her head in place, the ghost was seemingly laid.

Another spectral woman is said to haunt nearby Pont-y-Gwendraeth or, as it is more appropriately known, Pont-yr-Ysbryd, which means the ghost bridge. It was in the late thirteenth century that Lady Nest, the daughter of Elidir Ddu, Lord of Kidwelly, became embroiled in a convoluted love triangle between her cousin Gwladys and the knight Sir Walter Mansel. They had both fallen for the same man, but Sir Walter only had eyes for Nest. In a fit of jealousy, Gwladys arranged for her foster brother, a 'scoundrel' called Merig Maneg, to murder the man who had spurned her affections. He laid in wait near the bridge where the pair had arranged to meet for what they thought would be a secret rendezvous, where he shot Sir Walter with an arrow and flung his dying body into the waves. Nest leaped into the water after her love, where they both perished and were washed out to sea.

It is said that Gwladys and Maneg were haunted by Nest for the rest of their lives, and a veiled lady who has been seen appearing and disappearing on the bridge is thought to be her restless spirit. She occasionally lets out a high-pitched wail, which is said to signify the upcoming death of somebody known to the person who was unfortunate enough to hear it.

More recently, the ghost of a medieval soldier has been seen at the castle, while a menacing voice is said to ring out from a former prison cell. In 2016 a 'shadowy figure' made headlines after it was caught on camera peering out from behind the doors of the great gatehouse by a visitor.

Oystermouth Castle, Castle Avenue, Mumbles, Swansea

As darkness falls on Oystermouth Castle, one of Swansea's more mysterious inhabitants emerges from the shadows to peer out over the village of Mumbles.

Now in the care of the city and county of Swansea Council, it was in the thirteenth century that the Norman fortress became home to the wealthy de Braose family, who gave it a makeover more befitting their lofty status. One of their additions was a personal chapel, which has been named Alina's Chapel after Alina de Braose, the daughter of Lord Braose. She is believed to have been the driving force behind its creation, and it has been claimed that she still returns to the scene of her finest achievement as the oft-sighted lady in white.

Oystermouth Castle. (© TravelLiveLearn.com (CC BY 2.0))

The former keep at Oystermouth Castle. (© TeleD (CC BY-SA 3.0))

The trees behind Oystermouth Castle. (© Cadw (CC BY-SA 4.0))

The pillar inside Oystermouth Castle. (© Mark Rees)

A popular legend, however, would suggest an alternative identify. In 1879, Charles Wilkins wrote 'The Legend of the White Lady of Oystermouth Castle', in which the castle is in the care of Earl Neville, a particularly evil Norman lord. A worker called Hilda recalls how he imprisoned a monk whom he blamed for the loss of his men during an ill-fated expedition and abandoned him to starve to death in the dungeon. A young guard took pity on the brother and hollowed out several places in a pillar in which to conceal morsels of food. This only served to delay, rather than avert, the inevitable, but as the end drew near the man of God passed on these words to the sentry: 'if any good man or woman, free of sin, should come to the pillar, and pray there, and pace around it nine times, his or her wish would be granted.'

During an incursion to Ireland, the unscrupulous earl raided and burnt down a bishop's palace. Everyone was left for dead except a single captive, the bishop's niece, who was to be his wife on his return to Wales. She was desperately unhappy and treated appallingly by her new husband, but she put on a brave face in public, and her kind nature endeared her to those who worked in the castle. They named her the 'white lady' because of her pristine clothing, and in a bid to help her escape her tormentor, Hilda revealed the monk's prophesy. With nothing to lose, she decided to put it to the test while her husband was away hunting in Gower and crept into the dungeon in search of the 'wishing post'.

She followed the instructions to the letter, and was so exhausted by the ordeal that Hilda had to escort her back to her room. The next morning the old maid, who would later claim to have seen the monk appear that night, found her mistress lying in bed as peaceful as a saint. Her wish had been granted, although not quite as anyone had expected. She was dead and finally at peace.

In 1911, Jonathan Ceredig Davies wrote that the wishing post was used by lovesick youngsters in search of a sweetheart. While wishing for a lover, they were to walk around the pillar nine times while sticking a pin in it and looking at the wall, after which the lady in white would appear.

One paranormal investigator who put this to the test was Peter Underwood, who wrote that 'for me she did not oblige!'. But he did record testimonies from those who believed they had seen her in the grounds, and their descriptions would suggest that she came to a far more grisly end at a whipping, rather than a wishing, post.

In one account, during a family picnic a pair of children came across a woman sobbing behind a tree. Their father investigated and noticed that she was in floods of tears but made no sound, and when she turned to leave, saw that her clothing had been torn to shreds, with blood flowing from the lacerations marking her body. She disappeared as quickly as she had appeared, and a similar sight was also witnessed by a ten-year-old boy.

On another occasion, the sound of crying was heard by a young couple in search of a little privacy underneath a tree. They noticed a woman in white with her head in her hands, who walked behind a tree but did not re-emerge. A dog walker, meanwhile, once found his petrified pooch frozen to the spot and walked in the direction of its gaze. He saw what appeared to be a woman dressed in white on the ground, who rose on his approach and disappeared through the castle wall.

Powis Castle, Welshpool, Powys

Powis Castle is home to many ancient treasures, rare plants and, so the story goes, a rather persistent ghost who made one of its regal rooms uninhabitable for its guests.

Now in the care of the National Trust, the medieval fortress turned grand country mansion was built in the thirteenth century by Welsh prince Gruffydd ap Gwenwynwyn.

A watercolour of Powis Castle from *A Tour in Wales* (1781) by Thomas Pennant.

The entrance to Powis Castle from *A Tour in Wales* (1781) by Thomas Pennant.

It overlooks a renowned baroque garden, and was dubbed the Red Castle, or Castell Coch, due to its distinctive red sandstone exterior.

The property was bought by Sir Edward Herbert in 1587 and served as the family residence before passing into the hands of Clive of India's family following the marriage of Henrietta Herbert and Lord Clive's eldest son Edward in 1784. It was only a few years before they tied the knot that a local woman claimed to have 'conversed with the apparition of a gentleman' while staying at the castle, and the encounter was recorded by Thomas Wright in his autobiography.

The events took place in 1780, and the Wesleyan Methodist minister John Hampson, who personally interviewed the witness, described her as a 'sensible and intelligent person'. She made her living spinning hemp and line, and found her customers by going door to door. It was while looking for work that she paid a visit to Powis Castle, only to discover that the family were away at their London residence. She was instead welcomed by the steward and his wife, who provided her with a day's work and a bed for the night, but as she was shown to her room she was surprised at how many servants escorted her and how quickly they pulled the door behind her. She was equally amazed at how lavishly decorated the room was, appearing more suited to the gentry than a poor old woman, but nevertheless she prepared for bed and settled down to read her bible by the fire.

It was while reading that she heard the door open and saw a man walk in dressed in a gold-laced hat and waistcoat. He paused by the window for some time, staring contemplatively into the distance with his chin in his hand, before turning on his heels and leaving once more. Suspecting the man to be an apparition, it dawned on her that she might have been placed in a haunted room, a suspicion that proved to be well founded. The room had long been disturbed by an unknown presence, and the ploy was to see what would happen if the spirit came face-to-face with the God-fearing Methodist.

She got down on her knees and prayed for guidance, only for her prayers to be disturbed by the man's return. Frozen in fright, she remained motionless as the ghost stood behind her, before taking its leave once more. She prayed for the strength to confront the man if he were to come again and, third time lucky, when he reappeared she found her tongue. She turned to face her visitor and asked, 'Pray sir, who are you, and what do you want?' The stranger raised a finger and replied, 'Take up the candle and follow me, and I will tell you'. She did as instructed and was led along the passage to a small room which she was apprehensive about entering. Noticing her trepidation, he promised not to harm her and that she should closely follow his every move. He revealed a box hidden under the floorboards and an accompanying key in a crevice in the wall, and asked her to send them to the earl in London. If this were done, he would trouble the house no more.

The items were dispatched the next day and, with that, the ghost had, seemingly, been laid. Soon after the old lady received notice from the earl that he would ensure she lived comfortably for the rest of her life, a promise that he is said to have kept.

In more recent times, another ghost who doesn't appear to be leaving the castle anytime soon is the 'lady in black'. In *Ghosts*, Siân Evans writes of 'numerous sightings by members of staff of fleeting figures' in the Duke's Room at the end of the Long Gallery. Visitors have also reported being touched by an invisible hand, and on one occasion two people independently enquired as to the identity of a lady dressed in black who had been sitting by the fireplace.

The most active area would appear to be the ballroom wing, which houses a grand piano that has been heard playing when the room is empty and locked. The door has also been heard rattling, as if somebody were trying to shake it open, and when the piano was moved during renovation work it was found to have returned to its original position, despite the fact that the slightest of movements should have triggered the alarms.

Other reports of ghosts at the castle include a builder feeling the sensation of hands being placed on his shoulders, a woman in white in one of the bedrooms, and a 'headless horseman' patrolling the surrounding gardens.

Rhuddlan Castle, Castle Street, Rhuddlan, Denbighshire

Rhuddlan Castle was built in the thirteenth century as one of Edward I's 'Iron Ring' of castles. The fortress' unique design saw it gain a reputation for being impenetrable due to its 'walls within walls' defences, and if that wasn't enough to keep unwanted visitors away, it also gained a reputation for being haunted by a particularly nasty entity from Welsh legend.

Now in the care of CADW, the Grade I listed ruin stands on a strategically important site which was fought over by Welsh princes long before the King of England invaded. A popular tale attached to the castle is 'The Knight of the Blood Red Plume', which was passed on orally until 1802 when William Earle recorded it in his *Welsh Legends*. It tells of Erilda, the princess of Rhuddlan Castle, who was due to marry Morven, the heir apparent to the throne of Wales, in a union arranged by their fathers.

Ahead of the big day, she had a brief encounter with a mysterious stranger who wore a suit of black armour topped off with a blood-red plume in his helmet. The melancholy knight with piercing jet-black eyes was eager to be on his way, but from that day forth his memory haunted her every waking moment.

In an attempt to distract herself, she accompanied her father, Sir Rhyswick, on a royal hunting expedition. Her aim was good and she shot a doe with an arrow but, being only wounded, it fled and led her on a wild chase through the trees. By the time animal faltered the pale moon was high in the sky, and the princess found herself stranded in the forest. While searching for a way home, the man who had been plaguing her thoughts emerged from the darkness and agreed to escort her to safety.

He introduced himself as Wertwrold, a forlorn wanderer, and remained as a guest at the castle for several days afterwards. During that time their love reached fever pitch, but with Erilda's husband-to-be expected any day, Wertwrold announced his departure and left her with a parting gift, a gold ring, which, if she were ever in need of his help again, she had but to breathe on it and he would appear.

It didn't take her long to raise the ring to her lips, and the knight magically materialised. They shared a passionate kiss and, knowing that their union would never be approved of, hatched a plan to elope under the cover of darkness. The knight had a coracle waiting for them on the River Clwyd, but they barely made it through the gates before the alarm was raised. With pursuers hot on their heels, Wertwrold handed her a dagger for protection, and with the river in sight, she felt a hand grip her shoulder. As she turned to face her would-be captor, he ordered her to plunge the dagger into their heart.

Rhuddlan Castle. (© Llywelyn2000 (CC BY-SA 3.0))

The Knight of the Blood-red Plume from *Welsh Legends: A Collection of Popular Oral Tales* (1802).

Rhuddlan Castle. (© steve p2008 (CC BY 2.0))

The view from Rhuddlan Castle. (© steve p2008 (CC BY 2.0))

The outer wall of Rhuddlan Castle. (© Tanya Dedyukhina (CC BY 3.0))

It was only as she thrust the blade into her assailant's body that she looked into his eyes and realised that she had mortally wounded her own father.

The true horror was soon to follow. On-board the coracle her once noble partner laughed at her tears and revealed his true form, that of a hideous green-scaled demon whose sole aim was to ensure continued bloodshed between the feuding kingdoms of Wales. His final act of wickedness was to pierce her heart with his trident, before flinging her lifeless body into the water.

While this story might seem a little far-fetched and lacking in historical accuracy, it's interesting to note that the protagonists seemingly live on to this day, and a ghost that has been sighted in and around the castle is thought to be the heartbroken Erilda. In some cases she has been seen fleeing from a pursuer, who is presumed to be the demonic knight, and unearthly screams and an evil laugh have also been heard.

In 2016, the ghost of an archer was reported on the premises by the national press, complete with photographic evidence that claimed to show the spirit peering around a wall. The snap had been taken some twenty-six years earlier, but was only noticed by a grandfather while going through old photos of his daughters. He was quoted as saying that 'There's definitely something there. He has black eyes and his hands are in a position like he is drawing an arrow back.' Could these be the jet-black eyes of Wertwrold himself?

CHAPTER TWO

Haunted History

From ancient monoliths to industrial workplaces, tantalising remains of Wales' rich history can be found scattered across the land. These are locations that have bared witness to moments in time that forever shaped a nation, and many of them are still standing today. Some have been preserved as attractions and can be explored by the curious, and in some cases, it would appear that they are also holding on to some of their ghosts of the past as well.

Dolaucothi Gold Mines, Pumsaint, Llanwrda, Carmarthenshire

The pitch-black caverns of Dolaucothi Gold Mines were first mined for gold more than 2,000 years ago. It was an unforgiving workplace and, as such, it should probably come as no surprise that tales of legendary hauntings, along with more recent eerie sightings, have become attached to this historical landmark.

The hillside above Dolaucothi Gold Mines. (© Glen Bowman (CC BY-SA 2.0))

Carreg Pumsaint. (© Nilfanion (CC BY-SA 4.0))

Deep in the Carmarthenshire countryside, the vast subterranean complex was originally worked by the Romans, after which it was all but forgotten about until being rediscovered and reopened by a group of intrepid Victorian entrepreneurs. Work eventually came to halt in 1938 and the pit is now cared for by the National Trust.

A standing stone on the estate is known as Carreg Pumsaint, which means 'the stone of the five saints'. The four-sided rock is believed to have been used as a Roman anvil, but a more fantastical origin story connects it to a pilgrimage of five saints to the city of St Davids. Ceitho, Celynnen, Gwyn, Gwynog and Gwynaro had to pass Dolaucothi en route, but little did they know that an evil sorcerer was lying in wait. He was more than familiar with the holy quintet, having previously failed to entice them away from the path of God, and when he discovered that they were approaching his lair he seized on the opportunity to thwart their progress by summoning an almighty storm. With the wind and hail pounding their bodies, they were forced to shelter themselves by huddling tightly against the stone, which they rotated around until they were ready to drop. The strange indentations that can be seen on it today are said to have been caused by the force of their heads and upper bodies being pressed tightly against it. As they fell to the ground exhausted, their adversary swept them up and stole them away into his den, where they now sleep until the return of King Arthur, who, incidentally, is also said to be resting in various locations across Wales and will arise once more in the country's darkest hour.

A related story concerns a girl named Gwenllian, who was lured into the mines by the Devil to spy on the slumbering saints but, unable to retrace her steps out again, was doomed to spend eternity trapped in a cavernous limbo. An alternative version of the tale claims that rather than being a nosey parker, Gwenllian was a regular visitor who bathed in the caves' healing waters. On one occasion she went under the water never to resurface, and no trace of her body was ever found. She is now only visible in the form of a vapour or mist during bad weather, which materialises above the entrance of Ogof Gwenno.

A more contemporary ghost encountered in the mines is said to be a miner named Ned Lyonns, who met with a tragic end in the 1930s. The accident took place on a bitterly cold winter's day, when the tireless worker, who clocked up more than seventy hours a week, was lowered down to excavate a mine entrance. He was working alone and failed to notice that his candle was slowly extinguishing itself until he was left in total darkness. His cries for help went unanswered, and as the hours ticked by hunger and desperation forced him to act. Despite his better judgement, he attempted to scale the uneven rock face towards safety, and as he blindly navigated the rough surface he lost his footing and plummeted back to earth. It was only at the end of the working day that his dislodged boot was discovered, but his body was nowhere to be seen. He is now believed to make his presence known with yells for help, which reverberate around the works.

Llancaiach Fawr Manor, Trelewis, Nelson, Caerphilly

Llancaiach Fawr Manor has gained a reputation for being one of Wales' 'most haunted' heritage attractions, and its rich history might offer some clues as to the identities of the spirits who are said to call it home.

Llancaiach Fawr Manor and gardens. (© Ashley0690 (CC BY-SA 3.0))

Above: The side of Llancaiach Fawr Manor. (© Llancaiach Fawr)

Left: A candle-lit figure inside Llancaiach Fawr Manor. (© Llancaiach Fawr)

Haunted History

Stone walls at Llancaiach Fawr Manor.

Now open to the public as a museum, the Tudor manor house was originally built on the site of a medieval dwelling by the Pritchard family around the year 1550. These were troubled times, and defence was just as much of a consideration as creature comforts, a factor that is reflected in the property's sturdy design, which incorporates thick fortified walls and doors that could, in an emergency, be used to quickly lock down parts of the building.

The house was extended in the seventeenth century and this is pretty much how we see it today, having been carefully preserved to feel like it's still 1645 inside. This was a significant year for the family who, like many of the upper classes in Wales, switched allegiances during the English Civil War. Having been staunch Royalists who even welcomed Charles I into their home, they defected to the Parliamentarian cause, with Colonel Edward Prichard, who was supposed to be galvanising support for the king in the area, fighting against the monarch's men in his new role as governor of Cardiff Castle.

In recent times, paranormal groups have reported a wide range of phenomena in all parts of the house, which include such familiar staples as strange sights, sounds, smells and sensations. One of the more unique aspects are the voices, which are presumed to be speaking in the Welsh language and are always heard in the room adjacent to the listener. Whenever anyone goes to investigate, they switch to the next room along. Distinctive odours have also been smelt, such as the flowery waft of violets and lavender, and even roast beef.

The most active part of the house is said to be an upstairs bedroom, where the rustling sound of a lady's petticoats have been heard. The noise has been attributed to the spirit of a nineteenth-century housekeeper named Mattie (Martha), who some believe died in the room. How exactly she passed over remains a mystery, but it is thought to have been a deeply unpleasant affair, with one suggestion being that she burned to death following an accident. Some have claimed to have seen her in the room with them at night, sometimes accompanied by an icy chill, while the ghost of a Victorian lady dressed in white which has been spotted baking in the kitchen is also thought to be Mattie.

Others have reported a sudden feeling of sorrow engulfing them as they enter the bedroom, and in an article published by the BBC in 2018, Mattie's spirit is thought to have cast her melancholy spell over the captain of the South African under-21 rugby team. While the group were having a tour of the property, he 'just broke down in floods of tears with no explanation. As soon as he left the room again, he was fine.'

Another supernatural occupant who met with a tragic end is a young boy who is said to have plummeted 40 feet from the first floor in 1906. He now makes his presence known with the patter of tiny footsteps and by touching the living in a playful manner, such as holding their hands or pulling their hair. He would appear to be in good company, with the spirits of several youngsters thought to play games on unsuspecting visitors at all times of day and night. The grand staircase seems to be their favoured spot, where members of staff and the public alike have heard child-like laughter, felt their clothing being tugged, and have even seen a child materialise on the sixth step.

Full apparitions reported in and around the house include a girl who conceals her face with a hood on the steps leading to the cellar from the kitchen, the figure of a Victorian gentleman who walks the grounds, and a man who appears to be lost in thought, seemingly oblivious to those around him. It has been suggested that the latter could be Colonel Prichard himself, who is also said to be the cause of footsteps that are heard pacing over the dais in the great hall.

Plas yn Rhiw, Rhiw, Pwllheli, Gwynedd

Ghosts weren't the only things said to be troubling the residents of Plas yn Rhiw in centuries gone by.

The sixteenth-century manor house overlooks a picturesque harbour in the bay of Porth Neigwl, the ominous-sounding Hell's Mouth in English, an area that had something of a reputation for being a hotbed for wreckers, who would sink and loot ships in the nearby waters. Smuggling was also rife in this part of the Llŷn Peninsula, and it has been suggested that the property's location would have made it the perfect place to stash any contraband food and drink that came in through the port.

The house fell into a state of disrepair after the final occupants left in 1922 until three sisters came to the rescue in 1939. Eileen, Lorna and Honora Keating, along with their mother, bought and moved into the property, and set about restoring the once grand house and its wildly overgrown gardens to their former glory. There they remained until the last of the sisters passed away in 1981, and the house, along with the surrounding land, was gifted to the National Trust in memory of their parents. A plaque in their honour reads, maybe somewhat prophetically, 'There is no death while memory lives.'

The view across Porth Neigwl. (© Jeremy Atkinson (CC BY 2.0))

The most traditional of the ghosts said to haunt the property is a white lady, and one tale relates to the captain of a ship which ran aground in the seventeenth century. It was a stormy night, and as the skipper dashed to the house for assistance, his crew were set upon. Not only was their cargo stolen, but each and every member was killed, and when a suspect was apprehended for the crime, the captain remained as a guest at Plas yn Rhiw to await the trial. As he slept one night he suddenly awoke to find a lady in white in his bedroom, who beckoned him to follow. He did just that and was led into another room where she pointed towards a window seat with a large cupboard door. Upon opening it he discovered a body concealed inside, which, after investigation, was found to be a woman who had disappeared some fifty years earlier.

This isn't the only account of a white lady at the property. Another has been heard weeping at night in what is thought to have been her bedroom. According to the legend, she was the daughter of a Mr Williams, who owned the house for a while during the nineteenth century. Possibly named Annie, she fell in love with a 'tinker' who roamed the area, but their relationship was strictly forbidden by her father. Blinded by love, she agreed to elope with the boy and boarded a train for Bangor with the intention of crossing the waters to Ireland. It didn't take long, however, for the somewhat naive girl to find out the hard way that her father might have been right, and she was left abandoned to fend for herself. She is now believed to have returned home, in spirit form at least, where she pines for her loss.

Another entity said to be inhabiting the house is an alcoholic squire who drank himself to death in the eighteenth century. He is described in Marchioness Townshend and Maude Ffoulkes' *True Ghost Stories* as being something of a rogue, and his unearthly footsteps have been heard pounding up the stairs at night as he coughs and splutters his way to bed. This might indicate that the spirit is, as in life, still intoxicated, and similar footsteps have also been heard walking back down the stairs in the morning. Maybe the spirit has arisen with a hangover and is in need of a hair of the dog?

South Stack Lighthouse, Holyhead, Anglesey

In 1859, more than 800 people were killed people when a violent storm struck the Irish Sea. The 'great storm' sank 133 ships and battered ninety more off the coast of Anglesey, and those manning South Stack Lighthouse did what little they could to help those in peril.

One man in particular paid the ultimate price for his heroism, and his spirit, it is said, does not rest easy. Contemporary reports claim that he now makes his presence known by noisily trampling through the building, tapping at the window to attract attention and desperately shaking the front door as if someone – or something – were trying to gain entry.

The living can gain entry by navigating a steep descent down 400 steps towards the islet, before crossing the crashing waves over a bridge that links it to Holy Island. Heavy ghostly footsteps have also been reported on this approach to the lighthouse, as have strange cries and screams, although it's worth noting that the adjoining

South Stack Lighthouse. (© Hanno Rathmann (CC BY-SA 2.0))

South Stack Lighthouse. (© Darren Glanville (CC BY-SA 2.0))

Beacon of light. (© Smabs Sputzer (1956–2017) (CC BY 2.0))

Looking across the footbridge to the steep track up the cliff. (© Andrew ARG_Flickr (CC BY 2.0))

The crashing waves at South Stack. (© Smabs Sputzer (1956–2017) (CC BY 2.0))

island is home to an RSPB nature reserve, and the thousands of birds who nest at South Stack Cliffs Nature Reserve are probably more guilty for these sinister sounds than anything supernatural.

The lighthouse dates from the early nineteenth century and was built following a campaign for greater safety in an area notorious for shipwrecks. The green light was given for Trinity House to begin construction in 1808, and it was completed in just nine months from stone that was mainly quarried from the island itself.

The resident ghost is said to be a former lighthouse worker and their family roots can be traced back to the creation of the building. The first man at the helm was James Deans, who was succeeded by his assistant Hugh Griffiths. In need of an assistant himself, John Jones was handed the position and, after his death, was replaced by his widow Ann, who was more than familiar with running the lighthouse after fifteen years at her husband's side. Keeping it in the family, her son Jack would later take on the role, and it was this Jack who was working as second-in-command to keeper Henry Bowen that fateful night when the tempest struck.

On 26 October 1859, a hurricane-force wind forced the *Royal Charter* steam clipper to anchor in Welsh waters. It was making its way from Melbourne to Liverpool, but rather than taking the safer option of an unscheduled stop at Holyhead harbour, it persevered on its journey, only for winds blowing at more than 100 mph to smash it into the rocks off Porth Alerth in Dulas Bay. Four hundred and fifty people perished on that one ship alone and the gale was named the Royal Charter Gale as a result. Many of those on board were gold prospectors carrying their loot back to England, and some are said to have attempted to swim ashore with their gold strapped to their belts, which only served to drag them down that much quicker.

From his vantage point on South Stack, the keeper did his best to light the seas. Jack was elsewhere when the storm broke, and frantically made his way across the island to be at Bowen's side. As he dashed over the iron suspension bridge, which was replaced by a sturdier bridge in the 1990s, the wind-battered cliffs let loose a hail of rocks, one of which came cracking down on Jack's head. Blood poured from the wound as he stumbled to reach his destination, but the storm ensured that his cries went unheard. It wasn't until the next morning that the keeper found his comatose body crumpled outside the entrance, the very door that is now said to shake as if jolted by unseen hands. Jack didn't die that night, but his injuries were so severe that he passed away three weeks later.

While most of the paranormal activity at this beauty spot has been attributed to his ghost, other spirits are said to include playful children of which little is known, while the AA's guide to *Haunted Britain* awards it top marks – five out of five – in its 'haunted rating'.

St Fagan's National Museum of History, Cardiff

No place quite encapsulates the heritage of Wales like St Fagan's National Museum of History, which is home to more than forty historical buildings that have been relocated, stone by stone or brick by brick, from across the country to create a unique centuries-spanning 'village'.

In 2019 it was recognised by the Art Fund as the UK's Museum of the Year, and if there were also an award for the UK's most haunted museum, then it would have a pretty good claim to that title as well.

St Fagan's National Museum of History. (© Richard Szwejkowski (CC BY-SA 2.0))

Kennixton Farmhouse. (© Michael Gwyther-Jones (CC BY 2.0))

Oakdale Workmen's Institute. (© MostlyDross (CC BY 2.0))

Autumn at St Fagan's. (© Mark Rees)

Outside St Fagan's Castle. (© Mark Rees)

There have been countless reports of strange activity inside and outside the open-air museum's historical buildings and if, as some people believe, ghosts are attached to the buildings in which they lived their lives, then few places can compete with such a vast montage of once inhabited properties.

At the heart of the museum is St Fagan's Castle, a Grade I listed Elizabethan manor house that can trace its origins back to 1580. The house was donated to the National Museum of Wales in 1946, and members of staff have reported a full-bodied apparition walking within its walls, while eerie footsteps and disembodied voices have also been heard. In 2004, a press release recalled how veteran cleaner Tony Hughes not only heard his own name being called out, but also traditional Welsh folk songs being sung in the kitchen. In the gardens outside. The waft of sweet perfume has been smelt in the grounds, along with the sight of shadowy figures walking the lanes and lurking in the darkness. According to legend, one in particular is believed to be a seventeenth-century soldier who lost his life during the Battle of St Fagans. Having been seriously wounded, he rushed in vain to the holy well near St Mary's Church where he hoped to restore himself with its magical waters.

One of the first houses to be donated to St Fagan's was the seventeenth-century Kennixton Farmhouse. Relocated in 1951, the Grade II listed building originally stood in Llangennith, Gower, and its distinctive colour cuts a striking figure. The exterior is painted in a dark blood red, and the original paint is known to have contained pigments of red ochre and ox blood mixed with lime, which might have been a charm placed on it by the superstitiously minded occupants to protect themselves from witchcraft.

Other properties of note include Cilewent Farmhouse, which began life as an open hall in 1470, but was transformed into a stone longhouse in 1734. Partitioned to allow the cattle to sleep at one end and the humans at the other, sounds have been heard inside long after the building has been locked for the day, and an icy chill is felt as people enter the doorway. In the early 2000s, conservation workers reported finding the footsteps of children in the dust of its sealed-off loft.

The lively spirits of children have also been seen and heard at Llainfadyn Cottage, which was built in Snowdonia in 1762 from sturdy mountain boulders for the quarry workers and their families. At Melin Bompren Corn Mill, meanwhile, it is the workers themselves who seemingly continue to toil away, with the cast-iron nineteenth-century waterwheel said to spin all by itself.

Pen-rhiw Chapel has been a Unitarian meeting place since 1777, and on special occasions still holds services to this day. It might also hold services of a more peculiar nature, with *toili* (phantom funerals), which are often accompanied by the equally dreaded *canwyll corff* (corpse candles), said to take place there after night fall. Welsh folklore tells us that these spectral processions are a harbinger of a real funeral soon to follow.

CHAPTER THREE

Pubs and Hotels

The pubs and hotels of Wales have long been a welcome site for thirsty locals and weary travellers alike. With their roaring fires and frothy pints, they are a haven in which to unwind with friends, to relax on a holiday or, for many, simply as a place in which to earn a living. From the good times to the bad, they are establishments where memories are made, which make them ideal places to visit for anyone in search of spirits, of both the alcoholic and non-alcoholic variety alike.

The Castle Hotel, The Parade, Neath, Neath Port Talbot

The Castle Hotel in Neath began life as a coaching inn in 1695. It quickly became the go-to place for the great and the good as they visited the town, with Napoleonic hero Lord Nelson, along with his mistress Lady Hamilton, said to have stopped off for the night en route to Milford Haven.

One of the admiral's lasting gifts to the venue was the Nelson Room named in his honour, which also played host to sporting history when the Welsh Rugby Union were formed there in 1881. Another room that has been named after one of its famous occupiers is the Burton Room, where Hollywood royalty Richard Burton, who was born in nearby Pontrhydyfen, and his wife Elizabeth Taylor, stayed on many occasions.

When it comes to reports of hauntings in Neath, no writer has written as extensively on the subject as historian Robert King. In *Haunted Neath* he describes the Castle Hotel as 'arguably the town's most haunted building', and while it might have changed hands since his accounts were first published, he assures me that people are still experiencing the same 'frights' there.

Some of the spirits that have made repeat visits include a lady in a white robe who walks the corridors at night, and a lady in black who descends the staircase before exiting the main doors, which 'fly open' at her approach. An Edwardian boy has been seen by 'many people' playing in the Green Room, and Robert says he is 'not a naughty boy, just running around'. He appears in the vicinity of a hidden trap door that leads to an old kitchen beneath street level.

A rather unique ghost known as the 'headless cavalier' was spotted by a customer not known for his flights of fancy. As he read his newspaper one day, he noticed the feet of a fellow drinker sitting next to him. He lowered his paper for a better look and caught a glimpse of the man's body, which was attired as if from the seventeenth century. As he raised his eyes to the man's face, he realised that something was missing – his head. With that, his companion disappeared.

Pubs and Hotels

The corridors of the guest rooms are said to be permeated by a supernatural chill, and room sixteen in particular is thought to be the 'most haunted room in the hotel', where poltergeist activity has caused members of staff to flee. One theory as to the angry spirit's identity is a chambermaid who, having fallen pregnant to a huntsman who ignored her request to marry, committed suicide by hanging herself from the

The Castle Hotel. (© Mark Rees)

The corner of the Castle Hotel in New Steet. (© Mark Rees)

The area opposite the hotel, which was once the stables. (© Mark Rees)

The nearby Neath Castle. (© Mark Rees)

ceiling over the stairs in 1845. She has also been seen peering from the window that overlooks New Street.

The best day of the year to go looking for ghosts at the hotel would appear to be Christmas Eve, when a resident spectre is thought to join in with the festive spirit. In 1998, after last orders had been rung, the building was cleared of merrymakers ahead of the big day. The only two remaining occupants were the deputy manager and a fellow worker, and as they sat in the foyer they heard a commotion upstairs. It sounded as if somebody was running along the landing. Upon investigating they found that the doors to the bedrooms had been opened wide and all of the lights had been switched on. They searched the area but couldn't find a soul, and after turning off the lights and relocking the doors, alerted the owner. He arrived soon after with his dog for company, and they ventured upstairs together, only to find that the lights were back on and the doors were open once more. The dog became agitated and darted from room to room, yet still they could find no trace of anyone, living or otherwise. Two years later, on 24 December, the sound of footsteps were heard once more dashing along the landing of the empty pub.

The building once served as a stopping-off point for the mail coach and the stables and coach house stood opposite. This area has since been redeveloped, but the eerie neighing of horses and the clanging of the blacksmiths' hammers are still said to sometimes fill the air at night.

Penrhyn Old Hall, Penrhyn Bay, Llandudno, Conwy

Penrhyn Old Hall isn't called old for nothing. The medieval public house is said to be the oldest building in the town of Penrhyn Bay and, if the stories are to be believed, it could also be the 'most haunted' building in the town as well.

Standing in the shadow of the Great Orme limestone headland, the late fourteenth-century property is thought to have been built on the site of an

Penrhyn Old Hall. (© Noel Walley (CC BY-SA 3.0))

A drawing of Penrhyn Old Hall by H. Clayton Jones *c.* 1910 from *Llandudno and District in Line and Legend*.

Penrhyn Bay. (© Tom Bastin (CC BY 2.0))

eight-century royal palace and was originally known as Plas Penrhyn. For a long time it was home to the Pugh family, which included Robert Pugh of Penrhyn, who became High Sheriff of Caernarvonshire in 1561, before passing into the Coytmor family through marriage.

The Pugh family had their own personal chapel nearby, and an unusual legend surrounding this place of worship was published by Revd Robert Williams in 1835. It tells of how, many years after the Reformation, the family remained loyal to the pope and kept a Catholic priest on-hand to serve them and some of their neighbours. They didn't only meet at the chapel for pious reasons, however, and a plot was hatched there in order 'to put to death all the Protestants in Creiddyn'. Their scheme was foiled when the boyfriend of a servant girl grew suspicious as to the late hours she was being made to work and demanded to know what was going on.

He related the details to his master at nearby Gloddaeth, who set off with a troop to stop them in their tracks. Some of the plotters escaped including the priest who was believed to be the main instigator, and it was only by chance that he was apprehended when a man at sea noticed smoke emerging from the rocks at Rhiwledyn. He traced it to an almost inaccessible cave called Tŷ yn y Graig (house in the rock), where the ringleader was discovered and identified as Sir William Guy, although Guy is also named Dai or Davis in other retellings. He met with a grisly end, being drawn and quartered in a field below the house, but even then he didn't quite leave entirely. When the Coytmor family took ownership of the home they discovered an old trunk that contained a 'withered hand', a grim momento that is supposed to have once belonged to the priest.

Whether the priest himself still returns to this day is unknown, but some of the spectral visitors who have been sighted at Penrhyn Old Hall do have religious connotations. The Baronial Hall is said to be 'the most intense area of paranormal activity' in the building, and a monk has been seen walking through the room above it and patrolling the passageway. Another spirit that haunts the stairway is thought to be a descendant of the Pugh family, who was killed by her two siblings in a bid to stop her from marrying outside of their faith.

This bears strong similarities to another curious tale attached to the property, which dates from around 1685. The house was then occupied by a family with a son and two daughters, and the son went travelling abroad as young men often did at the time. Before setting off he left two items hidden on the property with which to identity himself if needed on his return, which were a needle inserted between the ceiling and a joist in the kitchen, and the tooth of a harrow driven into a pear tree in the orchard. His travels lasted many years, and by the time he arrived home he was little more than a penniless beggar. His parents had both passed away, and his sisters, who were now in possession of the family house, had assumed that their brother had also departed this earth. Taken aback by his appearance, they accused the man of being an imposter, but he could, of course, prove his identity by pointing out the location of the two hidden items. Still they doubted him, and not only was he thrown from the property, but he was flogged for his efforts.

Their neighbours had better memories and had no trouble in identifying the wayward traveller. They offered him a roof over his head, which he gratefully accepted, but soon after he mysteriously vanished once more, and this time he did not reappear alive. The suspiciously minded assumed that the sisters, who stood to lose the estate to which they'd grown so accustomed to, might have been involved in the disappearance of its true heir. If so, this might explain their sudden change in fortunes, for that once proud family were from that time forth 'cursed' and reduced to ruin.

The house was later occupied by a Mr Hughes, who also made a grisly discovery that might offer some closure to this tale. It was while building a limekiln behind the house that he found 'in a fissure of the rock, filled with soil ... a perfect skeleton'.

The Prince of Wales, Ton Kenfig, Maudlam, Bridgend

In the early 1980s, the Prince of Wales pub made headline news following reports that an organ had been heard playing by itself inside a locked room. The newspapers declared that it was one of the 'most haunted' pubs in the country and, despite the best efforts of the experts who flocked to Bridgend to investigate, the case remained a mystery. The global media attention might has died down since, but the eerie activity remains and, if anything, might be more active than ever.

The pub stands in an idyllic spot overlooking Kenfig's vast nature reserve, and the surrounding area is steeped in myths and legends. Directly opposite is Kenfig Pool, which is said to be bottomless and home to a sunken city, while the sand dunes that stretch as far as the eye can see also conceal a 'buried city', which was swept away by a suspected tsunami in 1607.

It was soon after this natural disaster that the town hall was built, which served as a focal point for the displaced community who were forced to move further inland by the encroaching sands. Now a listed building, it forms a part of the pub and is where the strange sounds were heard in 1982. One explanation for the phenomena is the so-called 'stone tape theory', a hypothesis that suggests that the walls themselves act

The Prince of Wales. (© Mark Rees)

The view of Kenfig from the pub. (© Mark Rees)

Inside the Old Hall. (© Mark Rees)

Looking out from the Old Hall. (© Mark Rees)

The car park at the Prince of Wales. (© Mark Rees)

as a primitive form of sound recorder and are replaying moments from the past for future generations.

In 2017, I spoke with then-landlord Gareth Maund, who described some of the events which had taken place under his watch. Far from being afraid of his night-time visitors, he preferred to refer to them as friends and not ghosts, and even said 'good night' to them before retiring. His personal experiences include witnessing strange mists of varying colours in the bedroom, which on one occasion was a 'white mist, the size of a person, tapping the door'. He has also noticed how dogs and young children appear to interact with invisible entities in the building.

Much of the activity is said to centre around the old town hall room directly above the bar, where people have had their ears pulled, faces stroked, and heard creaks like footsteps on the floorboards. A ghost that smells like 'rotten fish' is also said to follow some people around the room.

A repeated sighting is that of a spectral boy who stands by a cupboard, who is believed to have been a nine year old who was killed in an accident the nineteenth century. The room was used as a Sunday school at the time, and its founder, the wealthy resident Mary Yorath, would collect the children in her horse and cart to bring them to the service. It was on one such journey that tragedy struck, when the horse was 'spooked' and a child died.

Another historical part of the building is where the pub's toilets now stand. They were built in 1973 on the site of an old courthouse, from where the families of those on trial would have been pleading for leniency as the verdict was delivered. It is here that a 'little old lady', described by one witness as being dressed in 1940s style clothing, has been seen. She has been heard coughing and speaking, with one local hearing a voice saying 'I see you, I see you.'

In the bar area, members of staff have reported being touched and have heard their name being called, while in the kitchen jugs have 'shot' off the shelves at speed and shattered into the opposite wall. The main door leading into the bar is said to open and slam by itself, and did so with so much force one Christmas Day that Gareth expected it to come off its hinges.

He also had a chilling encounter just outside the pub after letting the dogs out. It was a perfectly cold, frosty night, and as he was waiting for their return he heard a voice shouting 'good night, Jack.' He recalled that 'it got louder, and after four or five times I couldn't get the dogs in fast enough.' He believes that the voice might have belonged to a farmer who used to frequent the pub and that the Jack they referred to was the name of a previous landlord who would have been in charge during their time drinking there.

Ruthin Castle Hotel, Castle Street, Ruthin, Denbighshire

Ruthin Castle Hotel is a romantic retreat set in acres of sprawling woodland. Just a stone's throw away from the River Clwyd, the hotel takes its name from the remains of a medieval castle on the estate, and some of the old tales surrounding this once mighty fortress might lend a clue as to the identity of the apparitions who are said to call it home.

Ruthin Castle courtyard. (© Neil Parley (CC BY 3.0))

Ruthin Castle gatehouse. (© Jim Linwood (CC BY 2.0))

Ruthin Castle. (© Llywelyn2000 (CC BY-SA 3.0))

Ruthin Castle grounds. (© Peter Broster (CC BY 2.0))

Originally known as Castell Coch yn yr Gwernfor (red castle in the great marsh), it was built in the thirteenth century by Dafydd ap Gruffydd on the site of an Iron Age hill fort. The land was gifted to the Welsh prince by Edward I during his conquest of north Wales but, when the country was firmly under English rule, his ally turned executioner. Dafydd was thus fated to enter the history books as the first nobleman to be hanged, drawn and quartered for a charge that would now be called high treason.

Another occupant of the castle who was equally disliked by the native Welsh was Sir Reginald Grey, 3rd Baron Grey de Ruthin, who was responsible for sparking Owain Glyndŵr's rebellion in the fourteenth century. He is said to have had a fondness for sadistically torturing his captives in the dungeons, and the names of some of his methods, such as the whipping pit and the drowning pit, leave little to the imagination. Footsteps have been reported following people in this former prison, while legend claims that by placing your arm through a hole in the wall you can shake hands with whatever diabolical entity dwells on the other side.

In the seventeenth century, the castle was reduced to ruin by the men of Oliver Cromwell during the English Civil War. What remains now serves as a dramatic backdrop to the hotel, whose more recent occupiers include Lady Randolph Churchill, the mother of Sir Winston Churchill. Accounts of its more supernatural residents, meanwhile, include a knight in armour, possibly one of Edward I's soldiers, who wears a single gauntlet and wanders the property oblivious to those around him. Another spirit, thought to be that of a young girl, is said to knock on the doors of the rooms as she runs through the corridors at night, where 'a glowing ball of light' has also been seen.

The most notorious ghost thought to prowl the castle's remains, as well as many other areas surrounding it, is the far-roaming grey lady. Named after the colour of her clothing, the most popular version of her story claims that she is the spirit of a fifteenth-century murderer who was executed and buried nearby. Something of a jealous lover, when she discovered that her partner, an esteemed knight and possibly second-in-command of the troops at the castle, was having an affair with a lowly working girl, she took her revenge by brutally butchering her rival with an axe. She was tried and executed for her crime but, as murderers were forbidden from being buried in consecrated ground, her body was interred just outside the castle.

A pile of stones are said to mark her final resting place, and her spirit has been sighted on numerous occasions walking a route known as the 'lady's walk'. The hotel's corridors are also believed to be a favoured haunt, while a 'crazed woman' brandishing an axe has been seen in the banqueting hall.

A more legendary tale of infidelity at the castle concerns King Arthur, who is said to have spent the night there with his mistress. When his rival Huail learnt of their secret rendezvous, he taunted the King of the Britons until he permanently silenced him by cutting off his head. The event has been memorialised on a limestone block in the centre of Ruthin called Maen Huail, on which is inscribed: 'On this stone the legendary King Arthur beheaded Huail, brother of Gildas the historian, his rival in love and war.'

The Skirrid Inn, Llanvihangel Crucorney, Abergavenny, Monmouthshire

In recent times, the Skirrid Inn has developed an almost legendary reputation for the sheer volume of paranormal activity said to occur there. It has become the go to for many a paranormal TV show, and countless visitors have experienced spooky incidents while spending a restless night there.

This wasn't always the case, however, and when Peter Underwood paid a visit in 1978, he found the pub deserted, and the only account of a haunting that he could trace related to a 'friendly' spirit mentioned in a newspaper article. The ghosts of the twenty-first century, it would seem, are far from friendly.

Wales' 'oldest pub' sits in the shadow of the Ysgyryd Fawr mountain, from which it takes its name. 'Ysgyryd' means 'shiver' or 'split' in Welsh, and the 486-metre tall landmark is also known as 'the great shattered hill', due to a legend which claims that it was shattered by a bolt of lightning at the moment of Jesus Christ's crucifixion. It became a place of pilgrimage for the faithful, as well as their great enemy, and folklore tells us that Satan himself would pay a visit to play cards with a giant on a plinth named Devil's Table.

The pub is said to date from 1110, although this may apply to an older building that once stood on the same site. The current property is thought to have been built mainly in the seventeenth century, yet many original features remain, including the medieval entrance doors, window frames and oak beams. These might have once been seen by Owain Glyndŵr who, according to legend, rallied his troops in the courtyard during the fifteenth-century Glyndŵr Rising.

The Skirrid Inn. (© Sandra Evans)

The sign outside The Skirrid Inn, which shows the moment the mountain was shattered by lightning. (© Sandra Evans)

The rear of The Skirrid Inn. (© Sandra Evans)

Pubs and Hotels 55

Right: The noose above the stairs at The Skirrid Inn. (© Sandra Evans)

Below: Fanny Price's grave (centre) at St Michael's Church. (© Sandra Evans)

A view of Ysgyryd Fawr mountain. (© Claire Cox (CC BY-ND 2.0))

Arguably the pub's most notorious period is when it is said to have doubled up a courthouse and those found guilty of their crimes were executed inside. The first man to be hanged at the Skirrid is thought to be John Crowther, who was apprehended with his brother James for stealing sheep. While his sibling's punishment was to be locked up for a time, John didn't get off so lightly. With a noose around his neck, he gasped his final breaths while swinging from an oak beam directly over the stairs. He was to be the first of many, and 182 people in total are claimed to have met their maker in a similar fashion. The hanging beam from which they swung remains to this day, with scorch marks etched into the wood said to have been made by the original noose centuries ago.

The man held responsible for many of these deaths is the notorious judge George Jeffreys, 1st Baron Jeffreys. Born in Acton, Wrexham, he developed a sinister reputation for the eagerness with which he dished out the death penalty and was dubbed the 'Hanging Judge' as a result. It was following the Monmouth Rebellion of 1685 that Jeffreys conducted the trials that became known as the Bloody Assizes, and as many as 700 people might have been executed for treason during this period.

A large number are said to have suffered a similar fate under his watch at the Skirrid, and his spirit is now thought to wander the upper parts of the building, as does his trusty hangman and some of their unfortunate victims. These include the ghost of a man with one eye, who took the extreme measure of trying to kill himself by stabbing through his own eye rather than suffer at the judge's hands.

Another regularly encountered spirit at the property could be a former barmaid or landlady. She makes her presence known with a sharp drop in temperature and the smell of perfume, while the sound of her clothing has been heard rustling by. Reports of a white lady, which may or may nor be related, are believed to be Fanny Price, wife of Victorian landlord Harry Price, who died in 1875 at the age of thirty-five. She is buried in the graveyard of nearby St Michael's Church, and historian Richard Felix writes that she is thought to have died from 'unnatural causes in bedroom number three'.

Poltergeist activity in the form of tables being moved, plates being smashed and glasses flying around have been reported in the bar area. On the stairs, visitors have heard the sound of a rope swinging, felt a tightening sensation around their neck and sometimes show visible marks of their ordeal afterwards.

Paranormal investigator Gemma Tredwin, who has spent many a night at the inn, says that there's a constant feeling of 'never really being alone' at the Skirrid. She believes that all areas of the pub are potentially 'active' and along with her colleagues has experienced something unusual in most of the rooms. Room two is a particular favourite, which 'can feel very comfortable and then change significantly'. On one occasion she asked a spirit to 'back off' from her companion, only for a can of hairspray to fly off the sink and narrowly miss her friend's face.

From this room they have heard sounds of movement in the bar below, including a piano playing and a woman's laughter. Sleeping has also proven to be tricky, with two 'sceptical people' witnessing a hooded shadow figure, while Gemma has been woken up there by a loud noise at 6 a.m. on most visits.

CHAPTER FOUR

Grand Mansions

There is much to admire in the stately homes of Wales. The extravagant rooms, the family heirlooms, the endless gardens, and the Gothic towers. There's also the odd ancestor or two, who are determined to keep an eye on their pride and joy long after shuffling off this mortal coil. Many of these far-from-humble abodes are lovingly maintained as attractions, which ensures that the grand properties from the past, along with any paranormal residents, remain frozen in time for all prosperity.

Craflwyn Hall, Beddgelert, Caernarfon, Gwynedd

Nestled in the shadows of Wales' highest mountains, Beddgelert is a legendary village with a legendary tale to tell. Its Welsh name translates as Gelert's Grave and it is said to be the final resting place of a heroic dog who was slain by his master in the thirteenth century.

The story, as recalled on a memorial in the hamlet, tells of how Llewelyn, prince of north Wales, returned home from hunting one day to find his faithful hound Gelert stained and smeared with blood. The dog has been left guarding his baby son and heir, whose cot he found overturned and equally bloodstained. Assuming that Gelert must have attacked and killed the infant, he lashed out with his sword and pierced the dog's side. He soon realised his mistake when 'the dog's dying yell was answered by a child's cry', whom he discovered unharmed alongside the body of a mighty wolf, which Gelert had killed while protecting the baby.

Sadly, or happily for dog lovers, this story is almost certainly a fabrication and is believed to have been invented by an enterprising landlord in the eighteenth century to drum up extra trade for his pub. It did the trick and is one of the many reasons why tourists still flock to the area today.

On the outskirts of the village is the sprawling Craflwyn estate which, after decades of neglect, has been restored by the National Trust. It wasn't so long ago, however, that it cut a much more unkempt figure, and became the scene of some rather unnerving ghost sightings, as recorded in the National Trust's *Ghosts*.

The land was inherited at the end of the nineteenth century by Llewelyn England Sydney Parry, a man of some wealth and standing who built a grand country house which would fill his guests with awe and envy. This he more than achieved and Craflwyn Hall flourished until 1895, after which successive owners struggled to get to grips with maintaining such an extravagant home and vast area of land.

A view of Beddgelert. (© Edward Crompton (CC BY-SA 2.0))

Gelert's Grave in Beddgelert. (© Peta Chow (CC BY 2.0))

Slowly but surely it deteriorated, but that didn't dissuade David Nemrow, a taxi driver from Manchester, from snapping up the property after winning the pools in the 1960s. He had a long-held ambition to live in the mountains of Snowdonia, and he and his wife were quite comfortable there to begin with. It wasn't until the 1990s that the constant drain on their finances began to tell. In a bid to save a few pounds they decided to lock up some of the less frequently used rooms. This left them with only the kitchen, the living room and a bedroom in which to live, while the garden also went uncared for and the overgrown plants cast their home into a permanent gloom.

It was under these circumstances, which were more befitting a Gothic horror novel than a dream countryside retreat, that the paranormal activity began. At first it was noises, which were heard on a nightly basis emanating from the locked rooms. Sounding like the appeals of prisoners banging for release, far from encouraging the couple to reopen them, they instead retreated further into their own little world.

It was while napping in the kitchen one day that Mrs Nemrow awoke with a start to find 'a handsome woman in a floor-length red silk Victorian gown' standing before her. The apparition, which she said was 'all shimmery', then 'slowly dissolved into thin air'. The spirit's face had been one that she recognised – it looked just like the portrait of Mrs Parry, the wife of the original owner and hostess to many a lavish gathering, which was hanging up in one of the locked rooms.

In 1994, with the house at its lowest ebb, the National Trust came to the rescue. A particularly keen young volunteer in search of conservation work was allocated the property and tasked with working the grounds during the daytime, while doubling up as security at night. He opted to sleep on a camp bed in the kitchen, one of the few habitable rooms left by the Nemrows, but was unable to get any rest. Loud noises, which seemed to come from deep within the house, ensured he was kept wide awake, while he was overcome by a 'sensation of creeping horror, as though some malevolent force was prowling the house'.

The next day he related his experiences to the property manager, who insisted that such noises and feelings were only natural in a ramshackle old building. To put his mind at ease he agreed to stop by to see him that evening but, upon doing so, was forced to eat his words: 'I have never felt such a spooky atmosphere in my life. The whole house seemed somehow poisonous, decaying. The volunteer was sitting bolt upright on his camp-bed, rigid with fear, not daring to close his eyes for an instant.' Unsurprisingly, the volunteer packed his bags and made a sharp exit the next morning.

If he were to return to the estate today he would be in for a much more pleasant experience. More than a million pounds has been spent on restoration work, and the sense of happiness, maybe not felt since those heydays of the Victorian era, has been restored.

Margam Castle, Margam, Port Talbot, Neath Port Talbot

Majestic by day and eerily atmospheric by night, Margam Castle is the jewel in the crown of Margam Country Park, a deer-filled nature reserve in the Port Talbot community of Margam.

It stands on sacred ground that was once a part of the vast Margam Abbey, a Cistercian monastery founded in 1147 that covered much of the surrounding area.

Margam Castle. (© Sian Burkitt (CC BY 2.0))

Margam Castle. (© Victor Ochieng (CC BY-SA 2.0))

Right: The stairs inside Margam Castle. (© Ruth Hartnup (CC BY 2.0))

Below: Margam Abbey. (© Hugh Llewelyn (CC BY-SA 2.0))

The grounds of Margam Castle. (© Hugh Llewelyn (CC BY-SA 2.0))

The discovery of Celtic crosses and stones on the land, which can be seen on display in the nearby Margam Stones Museum, hark back to the early days of Christianity, while a remote chapel overlooking the park called Capel Mair ar y Bryn (the chapel of St Mary on the Hill) is where ghostly monks have been seen gliding along the mountainside at night.

The abbey stretched as far as the nearby steelworks, where the 'cursed wall' of Port Talbot stands. Said to be protected by a curse cast on it by the last brother to be evicted during the Dissolution of the Monasteries, the hex states that if the wall were ever to fall, then the town would fall with it. Workers at the steelworks have also reported seeing spectral monks.

Remaining parts of the monastery can be found within Margam Country Park, and Peter Underwood, who recorded an account of visitors encountering even more ethereal monks there but in the daytime, described it as a 'place full of psychic power and undoubtedly, in my opinion, a very haunted spot'.

Margam Castle itself is, despite the name, not a castle but a Victorian country house. It was built in the Gothic Revival style for Christopher Rice Mansel Talbot in 1840, on land bought by Sir Rice Mansel, whose descendants married into the Talbot family, the wealthy industrialists after whom the town is named.

Now cared for by Neath Port Talbot County Borough Council, the most regularly reported spirit inside the property is the white lady, or *ladi wen* as she was originally known by the Welsh-speaking locals. She has been sighted making her way down the grand staircase, and there is a theory that in life she was Emily Charlotte Talbot, Talbot's heiress following the early death of his son. One of the wealthiest women in Great Britain, she followed in her father's footsteps by putting her own stamp on the estate and the town, and after her death in 1918 was buried in the family vault in Margam.

The ghosts of children dressed in Victorian clothing have also been seen, heard and felt inside the mansion. They are said to make a noise and brush against people as they dash about the rooms, while the spirit of a more reserved gentleman, also in Victorian garb, might have some connection with the little ones.

In *Ghosts of South Wales*, Steve Lockley writes that extensive renovation work carried out in 1995 resulted in a dramatic spike in supernatural activity. One theory is that the reopening of previously long-locked rooms might have disturbed a new batch of ghosts, seemingly more aggressive in nature than the existing inhabitants, such as one which hissed at people so violently that two members of kitchen staff refused to work there alone as a result.

A particularly angry entity who is believed to haunt the property is Robert Scott, a gamekeeper whose lifeless body was found on the nearby mountain in 1898. The Talbot family had tasked the thirty-nine-year-old with catching the poachers stealing from their land, and it was while on patrol with fellow employee Robert Kidd and private constable PC Hawtin that they came across a man acting suspiciously. The trio split up in order to circle the suspect, and it was while separated that Scott was fatally shot, first in the face and then in the body.

He was found in a gully the next day, which became something of a macabre attraction with thousands of people reported to have visited the grisly scene. On the day of his funeral work stopped to allow his colleagues, along with around 800 other mourners, to pay their respects. He is now said to make his presence known by slamming doors inside the property and furiously stomping around the grounds.

Newton House, Dinefwr Park, Llandeilo, Carmarthenshire

In a poll conducted by the National Trust, Newton House in Llandeilo was named as their 'most haunted' property in Wales and their fourth 'most haunted' property in the whole of the UK.

The Grade II* listed Jacobean house, which was given a Gothic makeover in the nineteenth century, stands tall at the heart of Dinefwr Park, a medieval deer park that has been occupied for some 2,000 years. The Grade I listed Dinefwr Castle, which is managed by CADW, can also be found on the grounds, as can the mythical White Park cattle, who are said to have grazed the Carmarthenshire grass since AD 920. According to the legend of the Lady of the Lake, who emerged from nearby Llyn y Fan Fach in the Black Mountain, they were to be a part of her dowry in her marriage to a local farmer.

Newton House itself is a magical labyrinth of grand rooms and secret hallways, and evidence of the superstitious beliefs once held by its inhabitants can be found in the form of a cat's skeleton concealed underneath one of the floorboards. Hidden from view, it faces to the east in order to protect its occupants from witchcraft.

Reports of ghostly activity from staff and visitors alike include the sounds of 'muffled men's voices' when alone in the rooms, lights being switched on and off after the building is locked for the day, and the lingering smell of smoke, as if somebody is enjoying a pipe or cigar. It has been suggested that this might be Walter Rice, 7th Baron Dynevor, and that the best time to catch a whiff of tobacco is while standing next to his portrait on a Sunday.

View of Newton House from the top of Dinefwr Castle. (© Glen Bowman (CC BY-SA 2.0))

Engraving of Newton House by John Preston Neale, *c.* 1820.

In a room at the top of the house, a motion-sensitive intruder alarm is said to be triggered when the room is empty at night. On one occasion a security guard was called to investigate in the early hours of the morning, and as they were waving their flashlight around 'the windows flung themselves open of their own accord'. Tour guide Ronnie Kerswell-O'Hara, who has witnessed inexplicable dark figures inside the house, was locking up one night and checked that 'the window was firmly locked into the frame'. When she returned the next morning it was wide open again, despite nobody entering the room.

These windows were in the former children's quarter, and a tale attached to the rooms might lend a clue as to the culprit's identity. In the 1720s Lady Elinor Cavendish, a relation of the lady of Dinefwr, was being pursued by a suitor that she was being forced to marry. In a bid to escape his attentions, she sought refuge in Dinefwr, which proved to be anything but a safe haven when her admirer arrived to reclaim his bride-to-be. She fled upstairs to hide in the nursery, but upon being discovered by her fiancé an argument broke out and, in a fit of rage, he strangled her to death.

Visitors have reported a sudden drop in temperature as they enter the nursery, as well as an icy chill in the corner of the room where she is said to have been murdered. Other reports include the feeling of hands being placed around the neck, while sightings of a white lady have been attributed to her spirit.

The ghosts of children are also said to haunt the property, and in an eerie portrait hanging at the top of the stairs on the first floor, youngsters who are no longer of this world can indeed be seen peering out of the darkness. The artwork depicts three of the family's children but when it was originally painted it contained five. Two of the children who died in infancy were painted over in black, only to reappear again under certain lighting conditions.

Another active area is said to be the stairway in the servants' area, which would have once been used to deliver food. One of those who now walks these stairs is believed to have been a butler.

Plas Newydd, Hill Street, Llangollen, Denbighshire

Plas Newydd was home to the world-famous 'Ladies of Llangollen', a pair of eighteenth-century spinsters who transformed their Denbighshire house from a humble dwelling into a truly remarkable Gothic mansion.

Lady Eleanor Butler and Miss Sarah Ponsonby eloped from Ireland to live together and found the perfect spot in a secluded Welsh town where they remained for more than fifty years. While never publicly confirmed, the pair are believed to have been in a romantic relationship together, and they quickly became celebrities of sorts, gaining a reputation for their distinctive 'manly' appearance, which included wearing a top hat on their short hair.

Their home became a stopping-off point for travellers as they made their way through Wales to Ireland, and those who spent the night under their roof range from royalty to romantic poets, including Lord Byron and Percy Shelley. They would ask their guests to bring a 'panel of carved oak or a curio' with them if they were ever to return for a second visit and, as a result, the house became dotted with a fantastic range of adornments, follies and stained glass. It also helped to stock their extensive library, which could be the most haunted room in the house.

Above: Plas Newydd with Castell Dinas Brân in the background. (© Stevieb3945 (CC BY-SA 4.0))

Left: Sarah Ponsonby and Lady Eleanor Butler, known as the Ladies of Llangollen, outside with a dog. Lithograph by J. H. Lynch, 1830s, after Mary Parker (later Lady Leighton), 1828. (© Wellcome Images (CC BY 2.0))

Above: A print of Plas Newydd as it was in 1840 by W. L. Walton.

Right: Plas Newydd façade.
(© Wolfgang Sauber (CC BY-SA 3.0))

Folly temple and font at Plas Newydd. (© Andy Dingley (CC BY-SA 3.0))

The best time to see the ladies' spirits is said to be Christmas Eve, although unusually they only appear to men on this day, while the most well-documented encounter with the duo was published by Dr Mary Gordon in her biographical novel *Chase of the Wild Goose*. While visiting Llangollen in the 1930s, she felt two 'presences' alongside her at Plas Newydd and, while she knew little of the pair beforehand, felt compelled to research their lives as a result.

Gordon soon returned for a second visit and this time encountered them outside the property, where they were dressed in 'light blue linen habits and fine muslin shirts'. She was even able to speak with them and, with so many questions to ask, they arranged to continue the conversation at 9 p.m. that evening in Plas Newydd's library. There was a snag, however. The house was derelict at the time, which meant that in order to keep her date she would effectively have to break and enter. Undeterred, she forced her way in through a window and the trio spoke at length until the break of dawn, with their discussion later published in the semi-fictionalised book.

Behind the property is Lady Eleanor's bower, which also has a curious tale attached to it. On 2 June 1829, the day of Lady Eleanor's funeral, a stray dog befriended the mourning Sarah Ponsonby. Having lost her long-time companion, she was in need of a little company and took the dog under her wing. She named it Chance and, on a visit to the bower, the dog howled inconsolably, which is said to have 'greatly upset' Miss Ponsonby. When Miss Ponsonby herself passed away on 9 December 1831, the dog disappeared once more.

The house is now cared for as a museum by Denbighshire County Council, who have restored it to resemble the ladies' original vision for the property. Many paranormal groups claim to have made contact with them, with a report published in

The Leader in 2010 describing it as a 'frightening place' where 'people were touched by unseen hands, knocks were heard in response to questions asked, an unnatural icy coldness filled the house, and faint voices and amazing light anomalies were captured on camera.'

Tredegar House, Pencarn Way, Newport

Tredegar House was once home to one of Wales' most notorious, and flamboyant, practitioners of the dark arts. Evan Morgan, 2nd Viscount Tredegar, had a seemingly insatiable thirst for the occult, and some of the reports of ghostly activity at the house might have some connection with his time at the helm of the property.

Now in the care of the National Trust, the Grade I listed red-brick country house is surrounded by 90 acres of walled gardens and can trace its roots back to the fifteenth century. Much of the mansion as we see it today was rebuilt in the seventeenth century by the wealthy and politically important Morgan family, later the Lords Tredegar. One of their more famous distant relations is the Welsh 'pirate king' Captain Morgan, the scourge of the high seas who is perhaps best known today as the character who graces bottles of spiced rum.

They welcomed many a high-profile guest to their Coedkernew home, such as Charles I of England in the seventeenth century, but it was Evan Morgan who took things to the extreme with his headline-grabbing high society parties in the first half

Illustration of Tredegar House from *Views of the Seats of Noblemen and Gentlemen in England, Wales, Scotland and Ireland. L.P* (1824).

of the twentieth century. Money was no object for the eccentric Welsh peer who liked to live life to the full, and one of his regular visitors was the occultist Aleister Crowley, labelled 'the wickedest man in the world' by the press. Yet even the 'Great Beast' himself couldn't compete with Morgan's appetite for the arcane and is said to have named him 'Adept of Adepts', the best of the best. Morgan gave himself the title the Black Monk, and strange practices were conducted in his bedroom, which doubled up as his 'magick room', and in the cellar.

One of the better-known ghosts connected to the property is the white lady, which appeared following the tragic death of Morgan's sister in 1924. The full facts of how Gwyneth Morgan lost her life remain a mystery, but what is known is that the twenty-nine year old spent her last days under close watch in London. Like her brother, the heiress had a reputation for being something of a party animal and, presumably as a result of the excesses of her lifestyle, was receiving medical supervision in Wimbledon. It was on 24 December that she walked out of the house unannounced, never to return. She had £70 on her person and was known to mix with some undesirable characters, and five months later her body was discovered floating in the River Thames. There were stones in her pockets to weigh her down, and while the official verdict was suicide, the suggestion that it might have been a drug-related murder persisted.

Soon after her death, rumours of a lady in white walking the house and grounds began to emerge. Gwyneth had not been immediately buried at home, and one theory is that the long delay in putting her to rest had caused her to wander in the afterlife. In *Haunted Newport and the Valleys*, the SWPR write that the servants at Tredegar House experienced 'feelings of unease and a chilling apparition of a lady in white' and that she was often encountered on a ground-floor staircase that connected to the Bell's Passage, an area containing an elaborate system of bells used to summon the servants.

A witness named only as Anne recalled an incident while supervising a class of children there on a school outing. The property was unoccupied and undergoing renovation work when the group, which numbered more than forty people, witnessed a bell violently ringing in the passage. Despite knowing that they were alone, they conducted a search of the connecting room only to find it empty. What was more puzzling is that they later discovered that the bells had been disconnected decades earlier when electricity was introduced to the property.

Anne also told of a friend's husband who had taken the job of security guard at the property. While not one to 'scare easily', after encountering a white lady while patrolling the grounds at night he was quick to hand his notice in the next day.

Other ghosts reported at the property include spectral nuns, which are thought to date from its time as a Catholic boarding school between Morgan's death and its purchase by Newport Council in 1974.

CHAPTER FIVE

Cultural Landmarks

Wales isn't known as 'the land of song' for nothing, and this strong connection with music, as well as the arts in general, can be felt in many of its cultural landmarks. From Victorian theatres to Elizabethan townhouses, these cultural hotspots have long inspired the likes of Oscar-winning actors and Romantic wanderers, and it would appear that some creative souls continue to draw inspiration from them long after the final curtain has fallen.

Craig-y-Nos Castle, Brecon Road, Pen-y-cae, Powys

In the nineteenth century, Craig-y-Nos Castle became the fairytale home of arguably the most famous opera singer to settle in Wales. In more recent times, it has become equally well known for reports of things that go bump in the night, many of which have been attributed to that same larger-than-life character.

The Victorian Gothic country house was built in the 1840s, but it was in 1878 that Adelina Patti bought the estate and transformed it into the grand mansion that we see today. The superstar soprano, who has been labelled the original diva due to her flamboyant lifestyle, made her fortune by commanding huge fees for packing out theatres around the world. Born in Spain to Italian parents, she could count such heavyweight composers as Gioachino Rossini and Giuseppe Verdi among her admirers, and on one occasion was invited to the White House by American President Abraham Lincoln to sing her trademark tune 'Home, Sweet Home'.

It was at the height of her fame that Patti went in search of a secluded spot in which to settle down away from prying eyes, and it was love at first sight when she came across the property in the upper Swansea Valley. She would remain at Craig-y-Nos, which she named a castle despite it being a house, until her death in 1919, and did much to endear herself to the locals by changing the face and fortunes of the surrounding area.

One of her more impressive additions to the property was a personal theatre, which allowed her to perform to up to one hundred and fifty guests, along with the servants who could watch from the balcony above. Now a Grade I listed opera house, the stage is decorated with a painted backdrop depicting Patti astride a chariot as the title character in Rossini's opera *Semiramide*, and one of its cutting-edge features is the mechanical floor which can be raised and slanted as needed. Beneath this floor is the backstage area where much paranormal activity has been reported, including objects being thrown and sounds being recorded.

Craig-y-Nos Castle. (© Dawnswraig (CC BY-SA 4.0))

The hills and mountains surrounding Craig-y-Nos Castle. (© Sandra Evans)

Right: Nineteenth-century print of Adelina Patti.

Below: The opera house stage.
(© Sandra Evans)

The opera house portico. (© Siaron James (CC BY 2.0))

Craig-y-Nos Castle through the trees. (© Ben Salter (CC BY 2.0))

Patti herself has, naturally, been assumed to be the source of many of these ghostly accounts, as have members of her extended entourage, including her second husband, the French tenor Ernesto Nicolini and, somewhat unlikely, the Italian composer Rossini who, while being a close friend, as far as anyone knows never actually visited Craig-y-Nos, or Wales for that matter.

The strange events which do appear to have a direct connection with Patti are those concerning her trademark song 'Home, Sweet Home', which was written by John Howard Payne for his opera *Clari* in 1823. It has been heard throughout the premises, despite no source for the singing being found, and in one anecdote a pianist who had never heard it before felt compelled to play the melody.

In *Welsh Celebrity Ghost Stories*, the soprano Elin Manahan Thomas recalled a time when she was recording a CD in the house. She would turn up early each morning to rehearse, and on one occasion could hear 'beautiful, dulcet tones wafting around the theatre'. Assuming it was her producer listening to some recordings, she made her way to the editing room, only to discover that it was empty. Nobody else had arrived yet, and she was alone. The sound seemed to emanate from the theatre, and as she made her way through the stage door the singing ended abruptly. When her producer eventually arrived, he found her 'white as a sheet and gibbering about dead opera stars'.

Towards the end of her career, Patti recorded a number of songs at Craig-y-Nos, and some paranormal investigators have attempted to communicate with the prima donna by playing these tracks inside the building. It is said to be a relatively successful form of communication, although Patti doesn't always respond favourably, and can make her feelings known in the form of angry poltergeist activity.

This could be due to the fact that the songs were recorded in her sixties and, as such, do not represent the singer at the peak of her powers.

Following Patti's death the building became a tuberculosis ward between 1922 and 1947, where children suffering from the deadly infection would line the rooms, and later a hospital for the elderly between 1959 and 1986. A large number of people would have died there during these decades, from those struck down in their youth to those naturally at the end of their lives, and this could be another explanation for some of the reported hauntings at Craig-y-Nos.

Plas Mawr, High Street, Conwy

Plas Mawr is a grand Elizabethan townhouse with a strong claim to being the birthplace of the visual arts in Wales. On top of that, it also has a strong claim to being the birthplace to some rather unique ghost stories, which have been reported at the property for centuries.

Plas Mawr gatehouse.
(© Stephen Colebourne (CC BY 2.0))

View of Conwy Castle from Plas Mawr. (© Tom Parnell (CC BY-SA 2.0))

Above and below: Inside Plas Mawr. (© Tom Parnell (CC BY-SA 2.0))

Exterior of Plas Mawr. (© Stephen Colebourne (CC BY 2.0))

Now in the care of CADW, the Grade I listed property was built in the late sixteenth century by Robert Wynn, a wealthy merchant who left his mark on the scheduled monument in the form of badges, crests and initials, which can be seen in some of the architectural details.

It was in 1881 that a group of artists, led by landscape painter Henry Clarence Whaite, set about establishing the Royal Cambrian Academy of Art to further the visual arts in Wales. Having been given the royal seal of approval from Queen Victoria, they settled in Plas Mawr where the academy remained until 1993.

It was soon after they moved in that two members of the public paid a visit to explore the artistic delights on offer, only to discover a little more than they bargained for. In a first-hand account published in 1893, the narrator recalls how an official working at Plas Mawr made the following off-the-cuff remark to the pair: 'Ah, you are studying the haunted room, are you?'

They laughed at first, but soon discovered that this was no joke, and that the haunting related to a concealed priest hole between the door and the fireplace. With their curiosity piqued, he explained that one night, while alone in the building, 'he heard a measured footfall begin to pace the room over his head'. He had also felt something 'pattering' around him at dusk, which brushed lightly against his body and made the sound of footsteps on the oak floor.

On another occasion, while walking with his wife in the courtyard below, he noticed that the window was open and 'saw something withdrawing quickly as he looked up'. He said nothing to his wife for fear of alarming her, but at supper she remarked that she had also seen 'something or somebody withdraw quickly from the window'. Similar activity was reported by others throughout the late Victorian period, and in 1897 it was claimed that the best day to see the ghost 'become visible' was on September 27.

An old legend which might provide some clues to the spirit's identity is said to have taken place on an autumn night at the end of the sixteenth century.

The lady of the house had some important news to share with her husband – they would soon be welcoming their second child into the world – and waited by the window with their three-year-old daughter for his return from the wars. As the hours passed and the night grew cold, she decided to quit her vigil until the next day, and gathered her child in her arms to descend the stairs. Then tragedy struck.

Losing her footing, the pair went hurling downwards, were they were found by the housekeeper who quickly moved them to the 'lantern room' and called for the doctor. Their regular doctor was unavailable, and so his far less experienced assistant Dr Dic was forced to attend in his place. Faced with the very real prospect that two high-profile patients might die in his care, he panicked and insisted that the main doctor be summoned immediately.

The housekeeper agreed but would not leave her mistress alone, and so locked the terrified assistant in the room while a servant was sent to locate him. The servant never reached the doctor, but the seriously injured mother and child did receive a visitor that night when the master of the house returned. A storm raged outside as he entered the room, only to met by a gruesome site: the dead body of his daughter, the dead body of his wife and, alongside her, the dead body of their prematurely born child.

He brandished his sword and vowed never to leave the room until he had taken his revenge. Despite there being very little Dr. Dic could have done under the circumstances, the frenzied knight wanted to take out his anger on somebody, and his mysterious disappearance made him the prime candidate. He paced the room and cursed until daybreak, but when the housekeeper entered in the morning all was silent. He had taken his own life, and lay next to his family.

Swansea Grand Theatre, Singleton Street, Swansea

At the turn of the twentieth century, Bram Stoker paid a visit to Swansea. The creator of Dracula was managing Sir Henry Irving at the time, and the actor, who is said to have inspired his blood-sucking count, was making one of his many appearances on stage in the city.

Whether the Irish writer encountered anything paranormal during his stay is unknown, but the spirit of a woman who has been seen, heard, felt and smelt at Swansea Grand Theatre is thought to have a close family link to the celebrated Shakespearian performer in his care.

There are several theories as to the identity of the woman, or women, said to haunt Swansea's flagship theatre, and in his book *Swansea's Grand*, Ian Parsons disproves one of the more well-known ideas that it is the ghost of the 'Swedish Nightingale' Jenny Lind. According to the story, she performed at the Grand before setting sail on the Titanic, the 'unsinkable' ship which hit an iceberg and saw more than 1,500 people perish at sea in 1912. His research revealed that Lind had actually died in Worcestershire in 1887, a decade before the theatre even opened its doors. An alternative version of the tale claims that it was a woman working in the wardrobe department who boarded the ill-fated passenger liner that day, having fallen for a touring American actor. She was on her way to join him across the Atlantic, and now haunts her old place of work where she first met the love of her life.

Another suggestion is that the ghost is the soprano Adelina Patti, who is more commonly associated with her former residence Craig-y-Nos Castle.

Cultural Landmarks 83

Above: Swansea Grand Theatre. (© Mark Rees)

Right: A poster for Sir Henry Irving's show in 1903. (© Mark Rees)

She officially opened the theatre in 1897, and the smell of violets, which are said to have been her favourite flower, have been attributed to her presence.

Perhaps the most likely theory as to the spirit's identity relates to the Swansea-born actor Mabel Lucy Hackney Irving, who married Sir Henry's son Laurence in 1903. She performed alongside her father-in-law in her hometown

The stage and auditorium at Swansea Grand Theatre. (© Mark Rees)

The first-floor corridor at Swansea Grand Theatre. (© Mark Rees)

A 'ghost' on stage at Swansea Grand Theatre. (© Fluellen Theatre Company)

annually from 1911 until 1913, and was due to return in 1914 when both she and her husband were killed when the RMS Empress of Ireland sank following a collision. On her final visit to Swansea Grand Theatre, she is claimed to have promised her wardrobe assistant that not only would she come back to perform the following year, but that 'When my performing days are over, I want to come back to this lovely town, and spend my evenings on the other side of the curtain, watching other people act.' Late in the evening of May 29, 1914, she made a surprise appearance in front of her dresser, and after saying that 'I told you I would return, but I can't really stay long,' made a sharp exit. The next day, the stunned theatre worker read in a newspaper about the accident which had taken her life – on the very same night that she had spoken with her.

An encounter with a ghost, possibly the same ghostly woman again, was recalled by former manager Vivyan Ellacott. It was on the night of April 20, 1968, that he and stage manager Philip Ormond were working late in order to get the next production ready. It was a particularly stormy night, and at 2am when they decided to wrap things up he noticed a solitary gas light was still on in the dress circle. He climbed the stairs and entered the darkened area, with Philip joking behind him that he should 'watch the ghost doesn't get you'. As he reached out his hand to turn off the light, he saw the switch move of its own accord, claiming that 'I swear it turned itself off!'. He felt a presence behind him, at first thinking it might have been his companion, despite there being no way he could have made it upstairs so quickly, and smelt the distinctive smell of lavender. He made a swift return downstairs, and noticed that his companion was also looking a little scared. They retreated to the safety of the car outside, where the manager explained what he had experienced, and Philip confessed that he too had seen something, for the briefest of moments, standing behind his friend, which disappeared as quickly as it had appeared.

Tintern Abbey, Tintern, Monmouthshire

Cutting a striking figure on the banks of the River Wye, few places in Wales have sparked the creative imaginations like the ivy-strewn ruins of Tintern Abbey.

Its secluded location was chosen by nobleman Walter de Clare as the ideal place to establish Wales' first foundation of Cistercian monks in 1131, and the Old Red Sandstone building that we see today is mainly the result of a thirteenth century restoration.

In the centuries which passed many a Romantic traveller visited to compose verse in its honour, and it is said that William Wordsworth was so inspired by the area that his 'Tintern Abbey' poem was formed entirely in his head before he even had time to put ink to paper. In the visual arts, the celebrated artist J. M. W. Turner was one of the many pioneering landscape painters to capture the masterpiece on canvas.

It also inspired many a ghost story, and a tale entitled 'The Troubled Spirit of Tintern Abbey' was recorded by Lord Halifax in his second volume of real-life spooky yarns. It had been submitted to the peer by a friend on the sole condition that he published it anonymously, and recalled a cycling holiday in the Wye Valley in the autumn of 1895, during which he and his wife became captivated by the abbey.

Tintern Abbey. (© Nevalenx (CC BY-SA 2.0))

Outside Tintern Abbey. (© Freddie Phillips (CC BY 2.0))

Above: Tintern Abbey. (© Angel Ganev (CC BY 2.0))

Left: The arches inside Tintern Abbey. (© Karney Hatch (CC BY-SA 2.0))

Tintern Abbey from the Devil's Pulpit. (© Nilfanion (CC BY-SA 4.0))

The first evening was fine, and with the moon high in the night sky they investigated the grounds. The narrator's wife was said to have psychic abilities, and was a dab-hand at automatic writing, a skill which allows the bearer's hand to be controlled by a spirit who might have a message to relate. While sitting on a block of masonry she put her powers to the test, and almost immediately her right hand was taken over by an unseen force. It tapped incessantly at her knee and, in a bid to make some sense of the communication, the husband proposed using a system with three taps for yes, and two taps for no. The response was in the affirmative – her hand tapped three times.

With a link established, they set about questioning the spirit by, somewhat laboriously, reciting the alphabet and allowing it to knock on the required letter. It claimed to be a Saxon solider who had fallen in battle nearby while fighting for King Henry II and, having been hastily buried without prayer, was doomed to wander the earth until Mass was said for his soul. The husband was sceptical, especially at the claim that a Saxon would give their life for a Norman king, but nevertheless they agreed to help.

The next morning he wrote a letter to a friend who was a Catholic priest, and on the last night of their visit they made a final stop at the abbey during which the soldier thanked them, via the wife's arm, for all that they had done. On their return to London they were surprised to discover that his claim of fighting for Henry II did appear to be genuine, and they also received a reply from the churchman who confirmed that yes, he did have the power to conduct 'Masses for the unknown departed', and would do so four times for such a troubled soul.

A decade later, a seance was being held at the couples' home for which they were joined by a pair of psychic acquaintances. As the session reached its crescendo, one final message began to emerge. The table tilted, and the following words were tapped out: 'Very many thanks for the Masses said.' At the same time, the two guests claimed to have seen something appear behind the wife, which they described as a 'bearded figure of a handsome middle-aged man, dressed in strange close-fitting clothes of a grey material'.

Another knight who is said to have appeared at Tintern Abbey was recalled in Frederick Ross' *The Ruined Abbeys of Britain*. The story begins when a group of men decide to meet in the ruins to get merry with food and drink, something which would have been deeply sacrilegious to the pious brothers who walked barefoot along its halls centuries before. All of a sudden, the sky darkened as if day had turned to night, lightning flashed above their heads, thunder shook the ground below, and a heavy mist engulfed the gang from all sides.

A glowing beam of light appeared at the entrance of the choir, and as it grew in brilliance they saw before them a 'mail-clad warrior, with visor raised, revealing a pallid and stern countenance'. He was surrounded by the many spectres of those holy men who had once called the abbey home, and as the storm momentarily subsided, he pointed his sword towards the doorway as if commanding them to leave. They didn't need to be told twice, and the 'defilers' ran as quickly as their legs would carry them. With that, the tempest returned with increased violence, and a whirlwind scattered the remains of their meal far and wide. It has been suggested that this was the spirit of Gilbert de Clare, 1st Earl of Pembroke who, like his son Richard, was also known as Strongbow.

More recent sightings at the abbey include a monk who kneels as if in prayer but disappears on approach, and a line of brothers who hold aloft torches. A news report from 2018 was accompanied by a photograph with claimed to show a cowled figure standing in front of the Great Abbey Church at night. There is also a rocky outcrop overlooking the abbey which is known as the Devil's Pulpit, and according to folklore is from where the Devil used to preach to the monk's below in a bid to stray them from their righteous path.

Wylfa Nuclear Power Station, Anglesey

A nuclear power station might seem like an unlikely place for a once-famous singer to be haunting, but that's exactly what was reported when workmen seemingly disturbed a dormant spirit on Anglesey in the 1960s.

Wylfa Nuclear Power Station was the second nuclear power station to be built on Welsh soil after nearby Trawsfynydd. Its location just west of Cemaes Bay was chosen for the abundance of water which could be used as a coolant, and it was in operation for 44 years between 1971 and 2015. It was during its creation in 1964 that reports of a ghost first emerged.

In August of that year builders from Ireland came face-to-face with what they described as a female apparition in a long white evening gown while digging the seawater tunnels. It has since been suggested that the woman in white they encountered was a prank played on them by a local worker, yet if a prank it was, it would appear to have been based on existing reports of a haunting in the area.

Sunset over Cemaes Bay. (© Huw Williams (CC BY 2.0))

Wylfa Nuclear Power Station. (© Andrew Woodvine (CC BY-SA 2.0))

Wylfa Nuclear Power Station. (© Tom Bastin (CC BY 2.0))

There were several sightings of a spectral lady from different groups of workers, and some of those on the night shift are said to have downed tools and refused to return after dark as a result. In one account she was heard as well as seen, and hummed a tuneful melody. Another report described her as an elegantly dressed woman who was standing on the edge of the cliff, but when they attempted to catch her attention she seemingly walked over the edge and vanished before their eyes.

The spot on Wylfa Head being excavated was once dubbed 'millionaires' row', and is where luxury homes would have welcomed the wealthy looking to get away from the city. One such property belonged to the internationally renowned opera singer Rosina Buckman, a soprano from New Zealand who settled in the UK where she later became a professor of singing at the Royal Academy of Music.

It was in the 1930s that she bought her Welsh holiday home, and visited regularly until she was forced to sell to the RAF during the Second World War. Buckman often invited her students along to join her and her husband, the tenor Maurice d'Oisley, for a break during the holidays, and to perform charity concerts for the war effort. It also became a favourite haunt of her mother-in-law Emma, who loved the area so much that she asked for her ashes to be interred in the garden, a request which was honoured following her death in 1935. It was there that they remained until the Central Electricity Generating Board disturbed them during the construction of the power station.

Some believe that the demolition work is what sparked the appearance of the ghostly figure and, after discovering the ashes and arranging for the casket to be buried once more in nearby Llanbadrig church, the ghost of Emma should, in theory, have been effectively laid.

Others maintain, however, that a strange figure still haunts the cliffs at night, and that it was not the ghost of the mother-in-law at all, but the ghost of the singer herself. In life she is thought to have had a favourite rock on the cliffs, which could correspond with the sighting on the cliff edge, and the ghost is said to be most active during the summer months, which is when she would have been enjoying her time there with her pupils.

In *Haunted Anglesey*, Bunty Austin recorded testimonies from some of the people who worked at the plant, which included security guards who were followed by footsteps, and who would find the lights turned on in locked rooms. In 1991, a night-shift worker saw an apparition from the canteen window which he described as 'a lady in a white evening dress, with long blonde hair over one shoulder ... looking steadily at him'.

Ian Clarke, who worked in the plant's reception centre, claimed that 'whoever the ghost is, she is not alone', and recalled a tale of a sinister male entity. It was while talking on the phone that he felt a presence watching him and, on turning, saw a 'tallish man, very dark-haired, with a very dark complexion ... wearing a white shirt, a (dark) waistcoat ... and a pair of buff-coloured breeches'. A cleaner called Christie also had several terrifying encounters the man, who was said to make a noise which sounded like a riding boot being slapped with a crop. She believed that he had followed her home, and both she and her daughter could hear the noise outside their bedrooms at night. Thankfully, it all came to end after she was moved to work in a different part of the power station.

A theory as to the ghost's identity was proposed by an 'older feller' called Tom Williams who, as a boy, worked on a nearby farm run by two sisters. The description matched their late father, a portrait of whom hung in the property. According to the story, in the Victorian era a 'pretty maid' went missing on the farm. She was found hanging from the clock tower, and it was classified as suicide. Those who discovered the body, however, maintain that she was strangled to death, possibly at the hands of her master, and that she was pregnant with his child at the time. Not only is the alleged murderer himself said to haunt the area, but the ghost of a woman who has being heard singing in Welsh is believed to have been his victim.

Bibliography

Alexander, Marc and Abrahams, Paul, *Britain's Haunted Castles* (The History Press, 2012)
Austin, Bunty, *Haunted Anglesey* (Gwasg Carreg Gwalch, 2005)
Barber, Chris, *Ghosts of Wales* (John Jones, 1979)
Coxe, Antony D. Hippisley, *Haunted Britain* (Book Club Associates, 1975)
Davies, Jonathan Ceredig, *Folk-lore of West and Mid-Wales* (The 'Welsh Gazette' offices, Aberystwyth, 1911)
Earle, William, *Welsh Legends: A Collection of Popular Oral Tales* (J. Badcock, 1802)
Evans, Siân, *Ghosts* (National Trust, 2006)
Felix, Richard, *The Ghost Tour of Great Britain: Wales* (Breedon Books Publishing, 2005)
Gordon, Mary, *Chase of the Wild Goose* (The Hogarth Press, 1936)
Halifax, Charles Lindley Wood, *Further Stories from Lord Halifax's Ghost Book* (Geoffrey Bles Ltd, 1937)
Hallam, Jack, *The Ghosts' Who's Who* (David & Charles Inc., 1977)
Jones, Edmund, *The Appearance of Evil: Apparitions of Spirits in Wales* (University of Wales Press, 2003)
Jones, Richard, *Haunted Britain* (AA Publishing, 2010)
Jones, Richard, *Haunted Britain and Ireland* (New Holland, 2003)
Jones, Richard, *Haunted Castles of Britain and Ireland* (New Holland, 2003)
King, Robert, *Haunted Neath* (The History Press, 2009)
Lockley, Steve, *Ghosts of South Wales* (Countryside Books, 1996)
Nicholas, Alvin, *Supernatural Wales* (Amberley Publishing, 2013)
Parry-Jones, D., *Welsh Legends and Fairy Lore* (B. T. Batsford Ltd, 1953)
Parsons, Ian, *Swansea's Grand* (Bryngold Books, 2010)
Poole, Keith B., *Britain's Haunted Heritage* (Robert Hale Ltd, 1988)
Rees, Mark, *Ghosts of Wales: Accounts from the Victorian Archives* (The History Press, 2017)
Rees, Mark, *The A-Z of Curious Wales* (The History Press, 2019)
Ross, Frederick, *The Ruined Abbeys of Britain* (William Mackenzie, 1882)
Sikes, Wirt, *British Goblins* (EP Publishing Limited, 1973)
South Wales Paranormal Research, *Haunted Newport and the Valleys* (The History Press, 2010)
South Wales Paranormal Research, *Welsh Celebrity Ghost Stories* (Bradwell Books, 2014)
Townshend, Marchioness and Ffoulkes, Maude, *True Ghost Stories* (Merchant Book Company Limited, 1994)

Underwood, Peter, *Ghosts of Wales* (C. Davies (Publishers) Ltd, 1978)
Underwood, Peter, *The A-Z of British Ghosts* (Souvenir Press Ltd, 1971)
Wilkins, Charles, *Tales and Sketches of Wales* (Daniel Owen and Company, 1879)
Williams, Robert, *The history and antiquities of the town of Aberconwy and its neighbourhood* (Thomas Gee, 1835)
Wright, Thomas, *Autobiography of Thomas Wright of Birkenshaw in the County of York 1736-1797* (J. R. Smith, 1864)

Online resources

anglesey-today.com
bbc.co.uk
dailypost.co.uk
huffingtonpost.co.uk
leaderlive.co.uk
museum.wales
nationaltrust.org.uk
penrhynoldhall.wales4you.co.uk
rhiw.com
walesonline.com

About the Author

For more than fifteen years, Mark Rees has published articles about the arts in some of Wales' bestselling newspapers and magazines. His roles have included arts editor and what's on editor for titles including the *South Wales Evening Post*, *Carmarthen Journal*, *Llanelli Star* and *Swansea Life*. He has written a number of books, with those of a supernatural nature including *Ghosts of Wales: Accounts from the Victorian Archives (2017)* and *The A–Z of Curious Wales (2019)*. In 2017 he launched the now-annual 'Ghosts of Wales – Live!' event, and in 2018 *Phantoms*, a play based on his ghost stories, was adapted for the stage by Fluellen Theatre Company and premiered at Swansea Grand Theatre.

Mark Rees. (Photo by Adrian White)